'The Rector will be Glad...'

A Norfolk Parish Miscellany 1898 — 1920

GW00643050

Compiled and edited by Susan Yaxley

First edition of 1,000 copies published and printed at
the Larks Press
Ordnance Farm House, Guist Bottom, Dereham, Norfolk NR20 5PF.
April 1992

Editorial © *Susan Yaxley 1992*

ISBN 0 948400 17 X

Preface

This book is a patchwork made up from extracts from that most humble and despised of publications, the 'Parish Magazine'. Part I, 'The Turn of the Century', has been mined from the pages of the 'North Walsham and District Parish Magazine', from 1898 to 1901. It creates a detailed picture of village life in Norfolk at this time, with the Church and its Rector at the heart of things, the parishioners more or less accepting the values they represented. There is much to admire in the village clergy, and some amusement to be derived, from the Rector of Mundesley, for example, who promises 'one word of advice' and proceeds to offer several hundred, and the Vicar of Gunton who is so horrified at hearing 'bad language in the harvest field'. Perhaps there is also a certain poignancy in realizing that this little world of Sunday schools, flower shows, cricket clubs and lantern lectures was the nursery for so many of the young men who later went off to fight in the Great War.

Part II, 'The Outbreak of War', has been compiled from the magazine of a group of parishes near King's Lynn, Grimston, Ashwicken, Flitcham, Castle Rising and Roydon, and shows how quickly many volunteered for war service and how soon parishes re-directed their efforts towards support for the troops.

Part III, 'News from the Front' is drawn from a remarkable and possibly unique publication, 'The Breckland Magazine' which existed for only three years, from January 1916 to December 1918. It was largely the work of one man, the Revd Charles Kent, and covered the parishes of Merton, Thompson, Tottington and Sturston. It contained, as well as normal parish news, extracts from letters written home by the men on active service.

The Epilogue contains items from the Garboldisham Parish Magazine.

Contents

— ✳ —

'Some Other Time'

by the Revd F. Langbridge, author of 'Songs in Sunshine'

If ever it should come about
That you and Tom seem falling out;
You feel your temper's got the slip,
And cutting words are on your lip;—
Or if you linger, half-enticed,
To tell some story highly spiced,
About the doings, wrong and rash,
Of Mr. Blank and Mrs. Dash;—
Why, here's a bit of homely rhyme
With counsel sage and true;—
Some other time, some other time— Some other time will do.

If Green, or Gray, who scorns to shirk,
Is down a bit and out of work,
And round his door, with hungry growl,
The gaunt old wolf begins to prowl;
And— though (with eggs at twopence each)
The ends don't greatly overreach—
You think, "I'll give a hand to Gray—
I really will — some other day";—
Why, here's a bit of homely rhyme
With counsel sage and true;—
Oh, Now's the time, the only time— No other time will do.

One wrote of old, a sage and king,
A time there is for everything;
For every work beneath the sun,
A season when 'tis meetly done.
For selfish folly, idle play,
The season is — Some other day;
For loving aid and service true,
Oh, Now's the time to me and you.
One word to close my homely rhyme—
An earnest word and true;—
There's little time, there's little time— And lots of work to do.

The Rector and his Flock

Picture the honest rector, sitting in his country rectory at the turn of the century, composing his entry for the Parish Magazine. He is a good man, living in hope and faith, regarding himself as a 'sincere friend and pastor' of his flock. The pen of righteousness in his hand, he sets about the dragons of apathy, poverty, intemperance and decay. Alternately lambasting and cajoling his parishioners, he tries to bring them to his church, to persuade them to pay their share of its maintenance, and to urge upon them the merits of a 'godly, sober and upright life'. The magazine goes forth, on to the kitchen table in the cottage and the hall table at the Manor there to be read with interest, hastily scanned or left unopened and eventually used to light the kitchen range.

Letter from the Rector of Mundesley

Mundesley Rectory, December, 1900.

Dear friends—

On January 1st we enter upon the 20th Century. I wish all my Mundesley readers a happy and bright new year. Happy in the highest sense, and bright on account of the realized presence of Him who has said, "Lo, I am with you alway, even unto the end of the world." In the first week of the new year I enter upon my fifth year of ministerial work amongst you. I have had a happy four years' work for the Master in Mundesley. As in everything earthly it is not all sunshine in ministerial work — there are many clouds of sorrow and disappointment over work done and individuals. But

Let me say one word to you who are fathers or mothers. I urge you most earnestly to realize your responsibility in the sight of God; your children are being influenced by you either for good or for evil. Is God's word honoured in your home? Is God's day kept holy? Do you so arrange your households that all can get to God's house once or twice? I thank God that so many men and elder lads do come to our old Church, but there are so many who I know go nowhere. There are some who come once in five weeks or less than that.

Young men and women, I beg you to put away all lightness of thought about our holy religion. Have the courage of your own opinions; break away from that so-called friend whom you know in your heart is not exercising a good influence over you. Why is it you are so backward in coming forward to acknowledge your King, the Lord Jesus Christ? I allude to confirmation and holy communion. Many of you have been confirmed; but why do you keep away from obeying your Lord's dying command, "Do this in remembrance of Me"? I ask you to be brave, to come out and make a stand, to give your hearts wholly and entirely to your Lord; thus you will cheer my heart as your pastor, and you will encourage and strengthen the hands of many a weak brother and sister.

Boys and girls, I most earnestly and affectionately invite you to strive to please God in everything; never let one word escape your lips that would bring dishonour to His name. Never neglect prayer. Tell God everything.

Your sincere friend and pastor,

T. Tegg Harvey

Attendance

At Dilham   Oct. 20th — Communicants, 6; Offertory, 5s. 9d
1901   Nov. 17th — Communicants, 5; Offertory, 3s. 9d
           Seeing there are about 220 persons in the parish of
an age to be communicants, and who profess and call
themselves Christians, the average attendance at the Lord's
Supper, which last year was seven, and this year as yet eight, is
sadly deficient.

The Rector very earnestly urges the husbands to give   **— and at**
their wives an opportunity of going to Church once **Mundesley**
or twice on Sundays. What arrangement could be   **1899**
better (where there are young children) than for the
father to bring the elder ones to church with him in the morning,
and then to have a quiet evening at home 'on guard' while the
mother goes to the service.

Deficit is feared at   At the Easter Monday Vestry, held in the
Ashmanhaugh   School, there was a miserable attendance
1899   (it *has* been hinted that people knew there was
           a deficit, and would be asked to contribute). The
out-going Churchwardens were re-elected. There was
a sum of £1 14s. 5d, due on the Beeston accounts, and 19s.
on those of Ashmanhaugh, but owing to the kindness of two or
three friends (who, by-the-bye, had already given) the accounts
were "squared." There must be something radically wrong with
the religion of a large proportion of professed Christians, when
their love to Christ and the carrying on of the work of His Church
is so shallow as not to touch their pockets.

Fabric and Furniture

New chimney at Bradfield 1899

A new chimney and cowl has been erected for the stove in the Church, which we hope will act properly and enable us to have fires at all times. Hitherto when the wind has blown from the coldest quarter the stove has refused to burn, and has shown its disapproval of attempts to light it by filling the Church with smoke. Now we hope that the new furnace will puff the smoke into the face of the wind and ask pardon for its rudeness when it has done its work.

Decay at Felmingham 1899

Our Rummage Sale on April 26th produced over £4. It is intended to expend this sum in endeavouring to make the East End decent and tidy. At present the Altar covering is moth-eaten and of the poorest material, the ornaments of wood, and the wall quite bare. We should be glad of help if anyone felt disposed, as the sum in hand is not sufficient. The Church has also had again a thorough cleaning. However poor we may be, we cannot expect reverence for God's house where anything in the cheap and tawdry style is considered good enough, and dirt and dust no disgrace.

New lectern for Crostwight 1898

Mrs Corner of Holmer Park, has very kindly given to our Church a handsome lectern of brass. The old little wooden lectern which bears a striking resemblance to a music stand, has been given to the parish church of Scoulton, which previously was without a lectern of any kind.

The Restoration of our Church has commenced, **Money** and services are now held in the chancel, which has **needed at** been boarded off for the purpose. At first it was **Smallburgh** only intended to undertake the internal renovation of the existing Nave, including re-flooring, taking down the west gallery, making the interior of the present roof more seemly — contenting ourselves for a time with chairs in lieu of oak seats. But when the gallery was taken down it was found that the west wall and the present ugly chimney tower were not quite safe, and this has obliged us to proceed at once with the further part of our Restoration Scheme, viz. the extension of the side walls of the Nave to their original length, and the building of a new west wall to look well by itself without a tower, but with the provision of a bell-cot. When this scheme is carried out it will remove a long-standing eyesore from the neighbourhood. It involves, however, an additional expenditure of £850, and we shall need all the help we can get to enable us to raise this sum. Donations ......

Poverty at August 16th, 1898 - On this day the Lord Bishop **Edingthorpe** of the Diocese visited the Rector in the Church. His lordship having looked around gave a short but expressive verdict, "It looks very poor." Alas! that verdict is true; and so long as the present English fiscal system continues, the verdict must remain true. The following figures may interest and perhaps edify some of the parishioners: The Rector succeeded the Rev. Joseph Lawson Sisson in 1891, since which time he has paid £211 16s. 1d. for parochial rates alone. Last year, for the Rectory of Edingthorpe All Saints', with an area of 710 acres and a population in 1891 of 183 (but now a great deal less), and with only *one* pauper in the parish, the Rector paid for so-called "Poor Rates" the sum of £35 3s. 8d. Add to these the sums paid for Imperial taxes, ecclesiastical dues, insurance, tithe rent charge on the glebe, repairs to the extensive buildings, house and chancel, man's wages, playing private charities &c., the parishioners, will easily understand that very little is left for the 'comely adorning' of the Church.

Subsidence at Tunstead, 1899 Those who were at the morning service on July 30th were startled to find that a large vault near the centre of the Church had fallen in, leaving a large hole exposed to view. This must have occurred that morning or previous night. Being in the central passage, the position is one of some danger. Forms are at present placed across. It is hoped that the wardens will be able to have it put right very soon.

'Test before you Trust' A tract bearing this title has recently found its way about Lower Horning. The first and last pages contain much that is good and profitable, but the inside is full of false statements about the Church, and misrepresentations and misunderstandings of her doctrine. We sincerely hope that all who come across this tract will follow the excellent advice given in the title, and "test before they trust" the statements it contains. In order to assist in this the Vicar has prepared an annotated edition of the tract in which the mistakes concerning the Church and the Prayer Book are corrected, and answers given to the numerous questions asked. He will be glad to lend it to anyone who wishes to see it, and we believe its perusal will be found not unprofitable.

Spiritual undermining at Horning 1899

A Lift from the Bells of Tunstead, 1901

The bells have been worked hard lately, and several recruits are being drilled, the Curate-in-charge among them. A few ærial flights have been taken, but no harm done under Mr Gower's able teaching. We hope to work up a full company again as in the old days.

Nuisances

Harriers at Horning 1899 A meet of the Yarmouth Harriers took place on January 9th — a pretty sight in itself, and pleasant, no doubt, for all concerned, except the hare. We regret, however, the action of the master of the hounds in riding into the churchyard and sending the hounds among the graves, and this after he had been informed that the hare had made off up the church field. We consider this a direct act of sacrilege, and an outrage on the feelings of the inhabitants, and we desire to record our firm and decided protest.

and boys A great deal of annoyance is caused by small boys running and shouting up and down the Mission Room loke, before and during the Sunday evening service. Will not the parents and others who have influence help to abate this nuisance?

Goings-on at Gunton 1901 As a notice to the youths who sometimes attend Gunton services and sit in the gallery, owing to the complaints of several of the congregation, the Church-wardens and the Rector have decided in the future no boys will be allowed to sit in the gallery, and it will be reserved only for the choir and Gunton Hall and any married people who prefer the gallery. If young boys think they can come to Church "to sit when they ought to stand," and consider the Church is a good place to eat "their dessert in," the Rector will turn out of Church any one he sees misbehaving at either Church.

Cross words at Crostwight The Rector was sorry indeed to hear swearing in the harvest-field during the recent harvest. How senseless and idiotic is the practice of using "bad language"! Let us never forget that "for every idle word that men shall speak, they shall give account thereof in the day of judgment." *Matt. xii. 36.*

Lightening the Load

Services in The Open Air Services in the valley near the hill
Roughton Valley commenced for the summer season on Sun-
1901 day June 9th. The attendance was good. On
the following Sunday the service was of a more special
character, when a most interesting and impressive address was
given to a large and attentive congregation by Mr.D.P. Anderson
of London. The afternoon was delightfully warm and fine, and
the valley presented a most picturesque and pleasant appearance.
Messrs. Wells and J. H. Hewitt with their violins contributed
much to the heartiness of the singing. We hope that these services
will continue to prove attractive to all who attend, and that many
find that the happy hour spent in the valley on Sunday afternoons
is a time of refreshing from the presence of the Lord.

A Church Army Van (Captain Cousens) **Church Army**
was in the parish from July 27th to August 10th. **at Skeyton**
Magic Lantern Lectures were given (by kind permission) **1901**
in Mr. Farrow's barn, and several open air services held in
different parts of the parish. We trust that under God's hand the
earnest work of Capt. Cousens and his assistant (Cadet Wallwork)
may bear good fruit. On behalf of the funds of the Church Army
an offertory was taken in Church, amounting (with additions) to
10s.

Rural Dean   On September 18th, the Rural Dean (Dr. Owen)
visits Crostwight   paid a visit of inspection to our Church and
1899   Churchyard.   He seemed very pleased with all
        he saw.   It is a difficult matter to keep everything always
in perfect order; but this is what we aim at.   An examination of
the Church Registers revealed to the Dean the fact that we had
had neither a baptism nor a burial for nearly two years; but with
a population which has now fallen below seventy this state of
things is scarcely a matter for surprise.   The Marriage Register was
new in 1837, and, according to the number of marriages which
have taken place since that date, it will not be filled up for the
next 820 years! But possibly the book, or the world, may not last
so long.

    The Rector has gone for a month's holiday to   **Stand-in at**
see if he can get better health and a stronger voice.   **Smallburgh**
During his absence the parish is under the care of   **1898**
the Rev. C. W. Formby, who is staying at the Rectory and
will look after your spiritual welfare.   The Rector asks for your
earnest prayers on his behalf.   The notice before the prayers for all
sorts and conditions of men will remind you of him.   We must
remember that our Church invites us to ask for the prayers of its
members when we fall ill, and not leave such asking until all hope
is past and they are dying.

            ...   .

    The Rector is home again, after five weeks rest at Lowestoft.
There were six fine days during that time, all the others being
cold, wet or dreary.   The Rector is better, but his voice is no stronger, alas!   He thanks the parishioners of Smallburgh for all their
good wishes concerning himself.

    [Revd S. A. Dudley Suffling died on July 30th, 1898.]

Schooling

Many parish clergymen had both a week-day Board School and a Sunday School to oversee. The financing of the village school and the provision of teachers for the Sunday School were a constant headache in some parishes, especially since the government grant to the Board School depended upon attendance.

Plundering the Ratepayers

As a member of the School Board the Rector wishes to call the attention of the ratepayers and parents of the children to the following figures:— During the last School year, which ended on June 30th, in addition to *nine weeks* holiday, the School was closed for 38 days by order of the Medical Officer of Health, consequently the School was open only 387 times a year. Not one child in the two parishes attended every time, and only three made more than 370 attendances, namely Lucy Steward (378), George Norgate (373), and Ernest Plumbley (372). Again, there are 93 children on the books, but the average attendance is only 68. This means that no fewer than 25 children are absent every time the School is open. It also means that the School loses at least £21 17s. 6d. in the Government grant, and £12 10s. for the Fee grant. Out of this large sum of £34 7s. 6d. the ratepayers in the two parishes of Paston and Edingthorpe are practically plundered by parents who are either too idle, careless or negligent to send their children to School regularly. No wonder that the School rate comes to about fourteen pence in the pound, and no wonder that the children make so little progress in their learning.— *George Sharley*

Poor performance at Tunstead 1899   The Rev. J. A. Laurence, Diocesan Inspector, examined the day school children in Religious subjects on June 26th. He gives the following general report: "The school has suffered from being closed for eight weeks in the spring through illness among the children. The writing out of the Catechism needs much attention, and the answering is not general enough throughout the school." It is a matter for much regret that not in a single sucject did the children earn a better report than "very fair". Of course the illnesses that so many children have suffered from during the last six months or so, are to some extent the cause of this, but still more so, is the lack of interest taken in the Sunday school. More teachers are wanted, who will set a good example in being regular and punctual in their attendance, besides taking a personal interest in each child. It should not be necessary, as at present is the case, that the Vicar and a day school teacher should have to take a class every Sunday. Another matter for regret is that all parents who have children old enough to attend do not cause them to do so, and that regularly, whether it be a church or chapel school.

The customary meeting of Ratepayers to elect school managers for the ensuing year was duly called for June 2nd, **Apathy at** but when the time came no one was present but **Neatishead** some of the retiring managers, who, after waiting for **1898** some time, went home with the understanding that there being no opposition, they might consider themselves re-elected. The accounts for the year have now been audited — they show, receipts, £225 15s. 9d.; expenditure, £221 10s. 2d.

One might be forgiven for thinking that rather more energy and enthusiasm went into the organising of treats and outings for the children.

On Friday, July 1st, by the kindness of **Knapton children**
Miss Hopper of Knapton Hall, the Board **go by train, 1899**
School children and teachers, numbering 54,
enjoyed the treat of a ride on the first train from
Knapton to North Walsham, returning in time to partake of
Mrs Cooper's hospitality before the hour for commencing school.

Sloley pupils Fifteen children of the upper standards, who had
go by tram made the best attendances at School during the
1901 year, were granted a holiday on November 1st,
and spent the day at Norwich, where, under the care
of their teachers (the Misses Sparrow and Watts), they
visited the Museum, the Cathedral, the Trades' Exhibition,
and also enjoyed a circular trip on the electric trams.

Tunstead School to the seaside by waggon

The annual Sunday School and Choir treat was held
on August 2nd. A start was made at about 9 a.m. from
the Church green, and the two waggons, which were
very kindly lent for the occasion by the Churchwardens,
Messrs W. Le Neve and J. Mack, were filled to overflowing
by the children and a few friends. Eccles beach was their des-
tination, this being an ideal place for such an outing, and all seemed
to thoroughly enjoy themselves. Soon after tea the return journey
was made. The day was gloriously fine. The thanks of all are due
to Messrs Le Neve and Mack for the loan of their waggons, and
the children have reason to thank all those who worked so hard
to minister to their wants.

School Treats at Swafield

1898 On January 4th the annual village Tea Party was held in the School and never before had there been so large a number or so sumptuous a tea. Ham and beef sandwiches and celery, bread and butter and cake abounded amid a lavish display of crackers. After tea Mr Walker entertained a crowded audience with sleight of hand tricks and ventriloquial sketches, which fairly brought down the house.

The boy who prepares for the Inspector

1901 Last month the annual School Treat was held at the Rectory. Favoured with beautiful weather and the presence of most of the parishioners, the event passed off satisfactorily. Cricket, sports, country games and swings were vigorously indulged in, and as every one tried to please everybody else, good humour and wholesome pleasure was the order of the day. Tea was thoroughly enjoyed by young and old, and all the more so because the ladies of the parish carried out the duties of attendants in first-class style. At the close of the day's proceedings cheers were given for the Rector and teachers after which the parting bun was given to each child.

The girl who is never late

Self-improvement & Healthy Recreation

The majority of village children left school at 13, but most parishes tried to make some provision for the young people to improve their education in various practical ways and to have some healthy recreation. Activities were clearly designed *either* for young men *or* for young women, and sports and games seem to have been regarded as a male preserve.

County Council Technical School at Mundesley 1899

A course of ten lessons will be given commencing in January 20th at the Royal Hotel, Mundesley, at 3 p.m. each Friday. All young women who wish to increase their knowledge in this most useful accomplishment are invited to attend the classes; the fee is one shilling for the course, or 1d. per lesson. There is no doubt that this is a matter too little thought of in many an English home: the digestive organs of children and adults are often impaired by bad cooking; the expenditure of housekeeping much increased by extravagance and waste through a lack of knowledge of how to cook up remnants of joints, vegetables, etc. It is said that our French neighbours are far more thrifty in the housekeeping department, through their skill in cooking. How many a young wife has scarcely any knowledge of cooking beyond the ordinary baking and boiling, and less about making good wholesome soups from the bones which are usually thrown

— poor cooking

away; and too often, alas! some fail even in boiling our humble friend, the potato, as it ought to be boiled, or in making a plate of porridge. These classes are a boon placed within the reach of all. The teacher will make and cook things in the presence of the members, and will explain as she goes on the "why" and the "wherefore".

The last Technical School Classes held in the village were to teach laundry work, yet (perhaps it will scarcely be credited) barely any young women of the village attended. This is remarkable when it is a fact that during the season visitors have actually a difficulty to get their washing done — they have to employ people from the surrounding villages. There are just a few, and only a very few, who undertake it in Mundesley. Surely this is a pity for so much money to go out of the place; but the visitors from London and elsewhere will have their things done well. If many of our young **— laundry** women attended such classes and learnt how to get **despised** up linen in high-class style, surely they would find the knowledge useful, even supposing they were never compelled to attempt it for a living. One instance came to the writer's knowledge which he has not forgotten: — A young woman was invited to attend the laundry classes, but she indignantly refused, as though it was beneath her to learn how to wash, starch, and iron properly; and yet she hoped soon to become a wife. The writer wondered if she would always be able to afford to put her washing out, and if not, how the husband's and children's shirt fronts, collars and cuffs, &c., would always look.

Let all who are interested take advantage of the classes offered at such advantageous terms by the County Council.

Carving with Miss Crump — Hanworth 1899

The Carving Class is now in full swing. Held in the Choirmen's room at the Vicarage every Tuesday evening at 7.30 p.m., many availing themselves of the kindly instruction of Miss Crump. Any desirous of joining the class must apply to the Vicar.

Young Men's Clubs

Gunton &   The first week in February a large room will be
Hanworth   ready at the Vicarage, where two bagatelle boards,
1899   draughts, books, and newspapers will be provided for
the use of the choirmen and boys of both choirs, on every
Monday evening. Two simple rules are to be observed — No bad
language or gambling permitted.

The School, which opens twice a week for the   **Too few at**
entertainment of the men, young and old, during   **Swafield,** —
the winter months, has not yet received that support
which it deserves.   The members that come are few, but they
appreciate the games and papers provided for them, and the hon-
orary secretary will be glad to receive the names of fresh members.

Too many at   The Vicarage Monday nights for young men
Worstead   promise to prove almost inconveniently popular.
1899   On the first Monday we mustered twenty-five, and
on the next thirty young men managed to insert themselves in to the room which without enlargement literally cannot
accommodate more.

Cycling Recommended by H. G. Wells

Mr H.G.Wells has discovered one of the chief charms of cycling.
He says:— "Its value is simply inestimable to nervous men, and I
think all writers are more or less troubled with nerves. There's
no time to think of anything when you are on the machine. It's
all nonsense for people to say that they think out stories and things
when you are cycling. It is just the simple fact that you are travelling so rapidly, and — however expert you may be — have to
mind what you are doing, which drives away all possibility of
thinking of work, and that is the joy of it. All the cobwebs get
brushed away from the brain, and you return to your work really
refreshed".

Cricket

Bad beginning at Trunch 1899 The Cricket Club has been started again for another year, but the general meeting of members took the form this time of a dinner in a public house, a bad beginning for a club.

In the match *v.* North Walsham on July 8th we were outplayed in every department of the game, and could only **Poor play by** make 36; Wade alone making double figures. **Gunton &** North Walsham Nondescripts, 196. On July 12th **Hanworth** our team was again beaten by Colby. Betts made 36, **1899** and Conrad Bankes 14. Gunton and Hanworth, 104; Colby, 184. Hanworth Club played Colby, on July 15th, and the match was lost by loose fielding, bad backing up, and a lack of discretion, though the Colby outfield was very rough. Scores not to hand.

We have to thank Mr. Wood, of Gunton Park, for kindly sending two bats for the use of the Cricket Club.

Recipes

For a sore throat Put into a jug a handful of dry sage leaves, two tablespoonfuls of salt, four teaspoonfuls of vinegar, and one tablesponful of Cayenne pepper; pour upon these a pint of boiling water, cover up close, and after standing half an hour, pour clear off through a bit of muslin into a bottle.

Harvest Drink A quarter-of-a-pound of flour oatmeal, six ounces of sugar, one lemon sliced, mix with warm water to a paste, and then add a gallon of boiling water. When cool the oatmeal may be strained off or left to sink to the bottom.

Charity — at home

Coals at Ashmanhaugh 1901 We imagine there are few parishes so well off in the matter of coal distribution as this. From the rents produced from the Charity lands the Trustees have been enabled to distribute a ton of coal to each cottager eligible. The Trustees are liable to be charged 2s. per ton for carting the coal from the station, but are relieved from the cost by the extreme kindness of Mr. S. Youngs and Mr. H. Mason, who give their waggons and horses and time free of charge. Practically, therefore, each cottager receives about 2 cwts. of coal extra and the least recipients can do is express their gratefulness to their kind friends. This does not always seem to have been done.

— and at Swanton Abbot The Trustees of the Poor met on December 12th and arranged the distribution of 245 cwt. of coal to the poor during the week before Christmas.
Widow Blackburn, to whom 12 cwt. has been allotted, died on December 17th and, her ticket having been returned, each of the remaining Twelve widows receive an additional cwt. this year.

Outing to Dilham Grange, 1898

On Monday, September 5th, the inmates of the Smallburgh Workhouse, between 30 and 40 in number, spent a very enjoyable afternoon at the Grange, Dilham, on the kind invitation of Mr. & Mrs. Heseltine, who provided conveyances for the women, while Mr. B. Harmer kindly sent the men in a waggon, and fetched them in the evening. Mr. Walker, the wizard of North Walsham, greatly amused the guests by his conjuring and ventriloquism, and gave them an appetite for a sumptuous meal of beef, mutton and ham, &c. to which they did ample justice.
A new meerschaum pipe with plenty of tobacco was given to each man, and a shawl to each woman, who all expressed themselves very grateful for the kindness shown them.

— and away

Children's help
at Westwick
1898
It may be mentioned as an encouragement to others, that by the children's efforts, chiefly by gathering acorns, they were enabled to send contributions for Children's winter dinners, Missionary Society, Christmas treat to crippled children, &c., besides brightening the lives of London ragged school children and others by gathering and paying the carriage of flowers.

Celebration at Trunch, 1899

The Centenary of the C.M.S. was celebrated on Sunday, April 23rd, by special services of prayer and thanksgiving. On Tuesday, April 25th, the children above Standard 1 were assembled at the Rectory and the weather, which had been threatening, cleared up at their coming. A map of the world had been traced on the lawn and the elder boys and girls, who had received some lessons in missionary geography beforehand, were furnished with little flags, which they set up at the principal stations of the Society. Other flags for other societies were also set up, and then a procession was formed about the lawn, the children singing as they went the beautiful hymn beginning "Let the song go round the earth, Jesus Christ is Lord".

The small figure represents the number of ordained missionaries in 1833, the large one the number today

The Demon Drink

The greatest, if not the only, social evil to be attacked in the pages of the Parish Magazine was the abuse of alcohol. The Temperance Movement was very strong and alcohol was denounced with every weapon to hand, factual warnings, lantern lectures and campaigns to restrict the sale of liquor on Sundays.

POINTS FOR THE TEMPERANCE PLATFORM

Consumption of alcohol
It is an extraordinary fact that the consumption of alcohol per head in the United Kingdom is greater today than it was in 1840. In 1840 the expenditure was £2 18s. 10d. per head: in 1898 it was £3 16s. 10½d.

Death Statistics
Within the last twenty years the ratio of mortality from alcoholic excess has increased 43 per cent. among men: but among *women* it has actually increased by no less than 104 per cent.

Public Houses
There are 156,102 licensed houses in the United Kingdom. Manchester has nearly 3,000, or one to every 180 inhabitants, Liverpool has 2,310, or one to every 279 inhabitants; while Birmingham has 2,300 or one to every 215 inhabitants. "The fatal facility of recourse to the public house" has greatly increased, making it "extremely difficult for multitudes of persons, in view of the hardship of their lives, to resist intemperance.

The Year's Outlay
The expenditure on alcoholic drinks in the United Kingdom in 1898 amounted to £154,480,943 a sum equal to one-and-a-half times the national revenues, or all the rents of all the houses and farms in the land.

Temperance Meetings

The first of this winter's gatherings of the **Warning at** Westwick Total Abstinence Society was held in the **Westwick** Iron Room on Friday, November 8th. Mr. E. G. Cubitt took the chair, and introduced the speaker, Alderman George White, M.P., who spoke of the success attending the Million Pledge Crusade Meetings throughout the country, and emphasized the fact that the work was as needed and as important in the villages as in the towns. He dwelt on the marked improvement in the poorer quarters of Liverpool, owing to the lessened number of public houses; and then gave a very touching account of a visit to Edinburgh. A night spent with a detective in the lowest lodging houses made him an eye witness of terrible scenes caused by drink.

Chemical demonstration
at Mundesley, 1899

Mr. Joseph Gray gave his most interesting lecture at the School on January 23rd to a large and appreciative audience of both old and young. The Rector presided, and after prayer Mr. Gray illustrated his lecture by chemical experiments. He very ably explained and showed the relative values of the constituent parts of bread, and compared the same with the constituent parts of beer (specimens of both he had in sealed bottles for inspection). He proved too, most conclusively, that alcohol was not an aid to digestion, for it had hardening and not softening properties. He showed lumps of sugar in alcohol which had been in the bottle for two years, and which rattled against the glass like stones. His manner was pleasing, and there was an absence of "intemperate language", which has done so much harm in the past to the Temperance cause. The following morning Mr. Gray gave a half hour's lecture to the elder children in the Board School — about seventy were present. He immediately caught the attention of the children by saying he was going to describe what was taking place within each of their bodies, with reference to the breakfasts they had just eaten. By means of a large coloured diagram and the help of a blackboard, he gave a deeply interesting lecture.

Referendum at Tunstead 1899   In connection with the Norfolk United Temperance Council, a canvas of all householders in the parish has been taken as to their views with regard to the stopping the sale of liquors on Sundays. Voting papers were left at each house by Misses Embling, Drury, and Bird. At the time of writing eighty-nine of these papers have been returned, leaving some eight more to be sent in. About six houses are at present unoccupied. So far, there are sixty-three in favour of stopping the sale, eleven are in favour of allowing it, and fifteen do not care either way, or will not sign. Of the eleven who would allow the sale, four are farmers, two tradesmen, one groom, one bailiff, three agricultural labourers. A complete classification will be given next month.

What Tobacco Costs. Before you boys think of beginning to smoke I want you to count the cost. We will leave health out of the question, and stick to pounds, shillings, and pence. Suppose when you are a man you spend one shilling a week — probably much less than you would actually spend. How much will that amount to in fifty years? Here is a table which you **Tobacco** can consult, compound interest being calculated **also castigated** half-yearly at seven per cent. per annum.

	£	s.	d.
At the end of ten years it amounts to	37	0	0
At the end of twenty years it amounts to ...	109	10	0
At the end of thirty years it amouunts to ...	255	10	0
At the end of forty years it amounts to	545	0	0
At the end of fifty years it amounts to	1,121	10	0
At the end of sixty years it amounts to... ...	1,772	10	0
At the end of seventy years it amounts to ...	4,999	0	0

Wholesome Entertainment

Local talent, like many another domestic commodity at that time, was spread thin and used thriftily. The same names tend to appear in concerts in several villages. Whatever the standard of performance, the parish magazine was determinedly encouraging and grateful.

Village Concert at Southrepps 1899

In November a concert was given in the Southrepps Board School, through kind permission, the proceeds of which were given to the Bradfield Church Improvement Fund. The weather was very inclement, and no doubt accounted for the attendance not being larger than it was, but those who were present spent an enjoyable evening, listening to the excellent vocal and instrumental music. Miss K. Amies opened the programme in her best style on the piano, and Miss Owen and Miss Musgrave charmed all by their sweet voices and power of expression; Miss Robinson, Miss C. Robinson and Miss Hopper carried the audience away as their nimble fingers tripped over the strings of guitar and mandoline; while the skilful manipulation of the harp by Mrs. and Miss Starling was most effective and delightful. Mr. G. Cobon sang to the pleasure of everyone, and Mr. G. W. Smith produced fits of laughter by his inimitable comic efforts. There is no need to speak of the "Gramophone," operated upon by the Rev. H. G. Corner, as it spoke for itself, but it brought to a conclusion a very good entertainment and one which brought to the fund £3 10s. 0d.

Easter Entertainment at North Walsham, 1898

An admirable Musical Entertainment was given in the Church Rooms on the evening of this day; and our best thanks are due and are hereby tendered to all our kind friends for their valuable assistance in making it the brilliant success that it certainly was. The net proceeds of the Entertainment, amounting to some £5, are to be devoted to the Repair Fund of the Church Rooms. The Programme was as follows:

Part 1 — Mandoline-Guitar Band
        "A Cuban Song", & "Chanson du Printemps"
Song - "The Deathless Army," Mr. H. Vulliamy
Song - "The Dreamers," Mrs. Kendall (encored)
Banjo duet - "Black Bess" Messrs. J. and E. Owen (encored)
Songs - "The Bugler" Mr. Glennie; "Asthore" Miss Owen
Comic song - "Tut, tut!" Mr. Vulliamy (encored)
Solo on the Post-horn - Mr. H. Shepheard
Part 2 — Mandoline-Guitar Band
        "The Enchantment" & "Cha-Chi-Pé"
Song - "The Gift of Rest" Mrs. Kendall (encored)
Recitation - "The Dream of Dionysius Boggles" Mr. Vulliamy
Song - "The Police Sargeant's Song" Mr. Glennie
Recitation - "A Short Address by Uncle Frank" Mr Shepheard
Trio - "The Wreath" Miss Owen, Mrs Shepheard, Rev. Thew
Comic song - "The Musical Box" Mr Vulliamy (encored)
Mandoline-Guitar Band   —   "God Save the Queen"

Horning Vicar out of pocket 1901   Mr. Brooks' entertainments on January 9th, both afternoon and evening, were excellent, and were heartily enjoyed by both children and adults.

Financially, however, the venture was not a success, the Vicar being out of pocket to the amount of 19s. 1d. Total receipts, £2 1s. 3d.; total expenses, £3 0s. 4d. We are much obliged to Mr. Porter for the use of his piano, and to Mr. Burckhardt, for pleasantly filling up the intervals with his violin.

New Technology

Cinematograph at Ashmanhaugh   On Tuesday, December 19th, there will be a grand Entertainment in Mr Mason's barn (that near his house), when Mr Coe, of Norwich, will exhibit the latest "Cinematograph," including such recent subjects as the departure of Sir Redvers Buller and the embarkation of the Scots Guards for South Africa. There will also be heard Edison's grand "Phonograph" (the very latest thing out), which talks and sings louder than the human voice, and gives band selections as loud as a real band. Tickets 6d, 1s., or 2s. (reserved).

Fleas and gnats perform gymnastics at Horning, 1898   On April 29th the Vicar gave a Lecture in the School, which was somewhat of a novelty in Horning. The lecture was entitled "Some wonders of the microscope", and was illustrated by a powerful lantern microscope, illuminated by the oxy-ether light, worked by Mr E. H. Stevenson of Norwich. A mounted specimen of the common flea was first thrown on to the 7-ft. screen, and increased from 15 inches up to 15 feet in length. Under the highest power only the head and legs could find room on the screen at one time. Several mounted transparent objects were shewn, including the blow-fly's tongue and the eye of a beetle, the thousands of lenses in the latter being plainly visible to all in the room. The greater part of the evening, however, was taken up with the exhibition of some twenty different species of live insects and other animals collected from dykes and ponds in the neighbourhood. These created much amusement by their lively antics on the screen. The palpitating heart of the water flea was very distinctly seen, as was all the internal anatomy of this curious little crustacean. The gymnastics of two gnat pupæ caused immense merriment, and the complicated jaws of the larvæ both of the gnat and the dragon-fly, were admirably displayed, as they were both kind enough to put their apparatus in motion for our benefit. [Proceeds after paying £1 5s. expenses, 14s. 10d for the Church Curtain fund.]

Church Rooms, North Walsham.

A MINSTREL ENTERTAINMENT

WILL BE GIVEN BY THE

North Walsham Black Diamonds

ON

Wednesday Evening, January 23rd

IN THE

CHURCH ROOMS, NORTH WALSHAM.

(By kind permission of the Rev. Canon Owen)

UNDER THE PATRONAGE OF

LORD AND LADY WODEHOUSE,

Chairman and Members of Nth. Walsham Urban District Council
Rev. Canon Owen, Rev. H. Wimble,
Rev. Balls, Rev. Corner, Rev. Gwyn, Rev. Key, Rev. Mercer
Rev. F. S. Thew, &c.,
R. T. Booty, Esq., F. Davies, Esq., J. S. Empson, Esq.,
Dr. Harrison, Dr. Hosegood, Major Ladell, W. W. Pallett, Esq.
Dr. Shepheard, and other gentry.

Stump Speeches, Comic Songs,
Minstrel Songs and Choruses,
Happy Darkies' Walk-round,
Witty Jokes and Dialogues,
Drawing-room Sketches, &c., &c.

BAND AND TROUPE OF OVER 40 PERFORMERS.

BONES—	INTERLOCUTOR—	TAMBOS—
Mr. E. T. Firmin,	Mr. A. Walker.	Mr. J. Falconer,
Mr. F. Press,	ACCOMPANIST—	Mr. H. W. Empson,
Mr. C. Frost.	Mr. J. Dixon.	Mr. F. Marjoram.

Doors open at 7.30. Commence at 8.

Plan and Tickets at Mr. Sutton's, Market Place.

It is recommended that an early application be made for
tickets, as a big demand is expected.
Ticket holders given first choice of seats.

Worstead Gymkhana 1898   We were favoured with the one thing wanting to ensure success for our Gymkhana and Bazaar, i.e. a glorious day; and the programme proved sufficiently attractive to bring a brilliant and distinguished company, who entered generously into the spirit of the gathering. Writing in the retirement necessitated by a somewhat serious accident to his knee, the Vicar can do no more than tender his heartfelt thanks to all who contributed by their hard work, and especially to thank his warden, G.Burnand, who was not only the Vicar's right hand but also his left leg.

A Poem found on the Editor's desk

I hear there are to be rare doings at Trunch,
On Wednesday, August 10th, after our lunch;
The men are to show both their dickeys and carts,
Lads are to run and do all them sort o' larks;
And the women are to take some home-made bread,
And sewing and knitting, so I have read;
Vegetables are to be sent in for show;
What have you got? Do you think you will go?

Taters and onions and cabbages green,
Marrows, lettuces and juicy pumpkin,
Carrots and cucumbers, parsnips as well,
Produce of all sorts, of which I can't tell;
All grow in my garden, at Swafield you know!

And I'm going to take 'em to the Trunch show.
What fruit have you got? Is that what you said?
Raspberries, gooseberries — as large as an egg!
And currants of all sorts, red, black and white;
Bless you! so big, I ne'er saw such a sight.
As to apples and plums, I can't crack a deal
'Cos I hav'nt enough to make up a square meal;
But with flowers and green food I'm quite satisfied,
And will walk 'em to Trunch if I can't get a ride.

National Events

The notice taken of national events depended upon the predilections of the Rector, and on the whole only the most important happenings find their way into the pages of the parish magazine, but the Vicar of Horning in 1899 drew attention to a forthcoming astronomical display.

Meteors

An event happens this month which takes place only once in every 33 years. On the nights of November 13th, 14th, and perhaps 15th, a great shower of "shooting stars" may be looked for. Unfortunately the grandeur of the display will be spoilt by the presence of the moon, which will be nearing the full, and for once we could wish the lesser light were below the horizon, that her rays might not interfere with the glorious sight which would otherwise have been presented to our eyes. It is probable that as things are, only the larger meteors will be visible. Whether visible or not, however, the fact remains that about November 14th, this year, and perhaps next year also, our Earth in her journey round the sun encounters what may be called a swarm of astronomical shot. These "shooting stars" are indeed solid masses of iron and other substances, weighing from fractions of an ounce up to several pounds. They come rushing at the Earth at the enormous speed of forty-four miles in a second, and were it not for the magnificent shield which the Almighty has cast round the Earth, we should be subjected to a terrific bombardment, for masses of metal would come to the ground in thousands, dealing death and destruction around them. As it is, however, these fiery darts are effectually quenched by the shield of the atmosphere, and the meteors enter the air from space some 100 miles over our heads only to perish in streaks of splendour.

DEATH OF THE QUEEN, 1901

At half-past six o'clock on the evening of this day, after only a few days' illness, our revered and beloved Queen passed peacefully away at Osborne, in the 82nd year of her age, surrounded by her children and grand-children. There was no protracted period of suffering, no struggle with ever-increasing weakness, no interval of diminished energy, to belittle in any way the grand perfection of her glorious Reign; and death trod swiftly on the heels of the first intimation that the ripe fulness of her noble life had come, and that the long work was at an end. In all her Reign of four-and-sixty years her joys and sorrows have been those of her people; and on this day, from end to end of the great Empire over which she ruled, a sob of sorrow made itself heard as the news spread far and wide, telling that the mother of her people was dead. Profoundly religious in thought and deed, a faithful wife, a tender mother, a pure woman, an ideal Queen, we "shall not look upon her like again".

Memorial Service at Hanworth and Gunton

On February 2nd, at 12 o'clock, the Memorial Service for our late beloved Queen was held in Hanworth Church, and at 3 o'clock in Gunton Church, at the time corresponding with the service held at St. George's Chapel, Windsor. The second form of the special services provided was used, and the hymns, "Peace, perfect peace," "O God, our help in ages past," and "On the Resurrection morn," were impressively sung by the choir. Both churches were nearly filled with very reverent congregations, many being visibly affected by the solemnity of the beautiful Burial Service; and doubtless to many it was a double memorial service, reminding some of those who had recently lost some loved one. The Dead March in *Saul* was tastefully rendered at each Church, and "O rest in the Lord," by Mr. Amies (the organist). At Gunton the Churchwarden had the altar draped in black. Any of the parishioners may buy a copy of the Memorial Service for 1d. if they wish to keep a memento of this memorable service.

Return from the Boer War, 1901

A very hearty reception was accorded to two of those who left our parish for the front in South Africa 18 months ago - Corporal S. H. R. Kidman, and Trooper C. T. Carman of the 43rd Imperial Yeomanry. Trooper Carman reached home on July 22nd and Corporal Kidman on the 23rd, and the welcome given to both was thoroughly homely, sincere and joyful. Triumphal arches of evergreens, made gay with flags, were erected, and many were the flags displayed in the village and carried by the school children. A supper was given to the men and their wives on both farms, and tradesmen connected with the Horning Hall estate, by Messrs F. Kidman and F. S. Carman. It was excellently served at the Ferry Hotel, and a large party of over 100 sat down. The Vicar had a very pleasant duty to perform after supper, in presenting some handsome testimonials: in the case of Corporal Kidman a gold pin, oak "tantalus" and dinner gong; and in the case of Trooper Carman, a handsome silver tankard and flask from his many friends in and near Horning.

'I KNOW A BANK' — by Frederick Langbridge, M.A.

There's a Bank that I hear about now and then
That takes deposits from working men;
It has shining mirrors and flaring gas,
And it draws its *draughts* in a jug or glass.
The customer there for his savings shows
A shaky hand and a flaming nose.
Keep out of its books, for I've come to learn
That Bank's a decidedly queer concern.

There's a Bank that I hear about now and then
That takes deposits from working men;
Its clerks are never too grand or fine
To enter a penny of yours or mine;
And the pence tot up, as I hear folks say,
To a nice little hoard for a rainy day.
Get one of its books, for I've come to learn
The Post Office Bank is a safe concern.

Local Tragedies

Tragic deaths in Northrepps well 1899   On May 6th the distressing news was brought to the village that two of our young men had been smothered by the falling in of the walls of a well in which they were working at Northrepps. The bodies were with great difficulty recovered after a week of anxiety and toil, and were laid to rest in the Churchyard on May 15th in the presence of a large assembly of sympathising neighbours. "Be ye therefore ready also, for in such hour as ye think not the Son of Man cometh."

Death of the Tunstead Organist, 1899

At the morning service on Sunday, May 14th, the Vicar had a painful task to perform, namely to inform the congregation of the very sad and unexpected death of him who for the last five years had been organist of this and S. Ruston Church, which had occurred at the Norfolk and Norwich Hospital the previous night. All the members of the congregation, the choir in particular, appeared to be shocked at the intelligence, and it was only with difficulty that the last hymn was sung. During the time that Mr Bishop has been connected with the parish, he succeeded in gaining the respect of all with whom he came in contact, and this in spite of his retiring nature and unassuming ways. The patience he showed in training the choir was inexhaustible. As an organ player and accompanist he was exceptionally good, indeed very rarely is one found with such a beautiful touch. However feeble the choir might happen to be he never drowned their voices with the sound of the organ. During the last year or so, he very kindly taught some members of the choir to play the organ and the violin. These members are particularly grateful to him, and feel his death sincerely. Although he had not been in good health for some weeks no one here suspected there was any danger of a fatal issue; he played as usual the Sunday before his death; in Norwich he played the very night before he died.

'Flu Deaths at Worstead 1898   On December 29th an impressive service emphasized our sorrow as we followed to his last resting-place, beneath the shadow of the Church which he had served and loved so well, the body of William Hannant, who, after a short, though painful illness, passed into peace on Christmas Eve. The choir was fully represented, and the spectacle as they met the mourners at the gate, and in long procession preceded the coffin to the Church, there making the responses reverently and distinctly and thence in their cassocks and surplices leading the mournful procession to the grave, where, in spite of a raging gale, and an obvious emotion which made all music difficult as they sang in sad farewell his favourite hymn, "Hark, my soul, it is the Lord", was one which no one would ever wish to forget.

The Church of Worstead has suffered sadly this Christmastide. We had scarcely recovered from the shock caused by the sudden death of Willie Hannant, when we were stunned to hear that John Grimes, who had started with the hand-bell ringers (after ringing the Old Year out and the New Year in on the tower) for their usual round, and gone home ill, had rapidly got worse, and within a week had died. He was followed to the grave by a large gathering of sympathising relatives and friends, and a muffled peal was rung in his honour after the funeral.

◆

Life-boat Disaster 1901   The Sermon and Collection for S.P.G. announced for this day were bound to give way to the particularly pressing claims of the above fund, which has for its object the making provision for the widows and orphans of the brave men who lost their lives by the capsizing of the life-boat "Beauchamp" on Thursday, November 14th. We record with pleasure the generous response made by our Church-folk in North Walsham to this appeal, a grand total of £20 11s. 8d.

Festivals

Rectors, churchwardens, squires and villagers came and went, but the three main village festivals, Easter, Harvest and Christmas were always celebrated in traditional style with the appropriate decorations in the church.

Easter 1899

The Easter decorations were undertaken by Mrs. Reeve, of Hanworth Hall, the Misses Chapman, Miss Oakely, and Mrs. Bankes, assisted by many of the choir girls and boys, who were very useful in obtaining moss and bringing flowers. The Church looked extremely pretty, and the decorations were beautifully executed. Mrs. Reeve was responsible for the sacrarium and altar, large pot plants of palms and lilies being arranged in corners and on the altar table, with a lovely display of white narcissi and arum lilies; the pulpit was decked with daffodils, also done by Mrs. Reeve and her helpers. Miss Oakely arranged the lectern and reading desk; the Misses Chapman and Miss Perkes very beautifully decorated the font, with a large cross of daffodils in the centre, and moss and pot plants at the base (quite a work of art); Mrs. Bankes decorated the windows with moss, primroses, and daffodils, assisted by E. Pratt, Peggs, Pitcher, Green &c. Mrs. A. Gibbons also sent flowers. The services were well rendered, and it was truly a gratifying fact to see Hanworth Church nearly full.

Harvest
at Hanworth
1899

Hanworth Harvest Thanksgiving Service was held on October 13th at 7.30, the special preacher being the Rev. J. Trendell, Vicar of Sprowston.

Many have heard Mr. Trendell before, and we were glad to have him preach to us on this occasion. As at Gunton we were favoured with lovely weather, a very good congregation, an excellent service (the choir rendering the hymns and Psalms well), and, we are glad to add, a good offertory. The Church looked very pretty indeed, lending itself, as it does, to decorations; and our best thanks are due to all those who so kindly sent their gifts of flowers, corn, vegetables and fruit, and for assisting to decorate. The altar table and sacrarium, as well as the pulpit, were beautifully executed by Mrs. Reeve and her helpers, in white chrysanthemums and pot plants. The reading desk, lectern, windows, and lamp pillars were most tastefully decorated by Miss Suffling and her assistants and friends. The font was very prettily decorated with white flowers floating on the water, and flowers and vegetables round the base. Mr. Bacon sent two very fine gourds, the largest we have ever seen.

On Christmas Eve carols were sung as usual at thirty-two stations in the parish, but we had this year to contend with a good deal of noisy and senseless opposition from some who ought to have known better, but who seem to think that the time of the Saviour's birth is an excuse for making night hideous with drunken and blasphemous uproar. The custom of singing carols on Christmas Eve originated in the carol sung by the angels to the shepherds. It is therefore a custom to be kept up and carried out as reverently as possible. We fear that owing to this unkind and unchristian behaviour several were unable to hear us this year, but those who were thus disappointed, and who expressed some indignation at the reason, were kind enough to send their donations all the same.

An
unruly
element at
Horning
1901

Part II — The Outbreak of War

A United Front

Reaction to the declaration of war on Germany in August 1914 was immediate in even the smallest villages. Some activities ceased for the duration of the war. Young men enlisted. Women began to organize themselves to support the armed services and nurses in every possible way, but chiefly by money-raising, and by knitting and sewing.

Castle Rising and Roydon

Little did we think when we went to press on July 21st, that by Aug. 4th we should be at war with Germany. But here we are to-day in the midst of it. Seven nations fighting for existence. Great Britain, France, Russia, Belgium and Servia against Germany and Austria. Twelve million soldiers at a cost of twelve million pounds a day. Three million square miles given over to war. It is the biggest war that has ever taken place in the history of the world. Every able-bodied man that can be spared will be required to defend his country under arms. And those who cannot do so must keep cool in the face of much anxiety, loss and disappointment, and go steadily about their appointed tasks.

The Royal Freebridge Lynn Association
for Rewarding Skilled Labour
Patron: His Majesty the King

We are requested to inform readers that no prizes will be offered for competition, nor will a show be held this year. 12th Aug. 1914

Ashwicken

NOTICE: A service of Intercession to Almighty God, that He may protect us against our enemies, and soon bring peace again, is held every day in our Church at 5 p.m.

Enlistment at Grimston

The war has taken 19 Grimston men for the King's forces, viz. four for the Yeomanry, five for the Special Reservists, eight for the Territorials; two Grimston men also are serving in His Majesty's Fleet. Very sincerely we trust that if any of these are called to the front — some of them no doubt will be — that they will return in safety, when the war is over. That they will all do their duty manfully, whether abroad or at home, we may be fully assured.

Letter from the Bishop

The Palace, Norwich,
September, 1914.

My dear People,

I am writing to ask you to help me in a matter which is near my heart. We know that it is always our duty to keep our bodies in temperance, soberness and chastity; at this time of stress the duty comes specially home to us one by one, and every claim of patriotism and sympathy calls us to help our soldiers in this direction.

I would be so grateful if you would personally do all you can by the grace of God in this way, and would also try to shield our soldiers and all our young people from temptation. Much harm can be done by good-humoured but thoughtless treating, and by allowing the young men and girls to be exposed to dangers together. Believe me to be,

Your Friend and Bishop,

B. NORWIC.

Entertainment at Grimston Rectory

On Monday, July 27th a very successful effort was made to obtain funds for the Congham and Grimston Nursing Association. This consisted in the giving a Pastoral Play in the Rectory Garden. There were two performances, one in the afternoon and another in the evening. The afternoon performance was well attended, many coming from quite a long distance. The evening performance, which of course was intended more for our residents, was not so well attended It had been hoped that many more would have been present, in spite of the fact that the charges were 1s. 6d. and 1s. Two pieces were given:— a duologue entitled "The Impertinence of the Creature" and a play entitled "The Error of his Way". Great pains had been taken to provide a suitable background and setting, and the audience were seated under the famous copper beech. The acting was perfect and gave intense pleasure. We had also the advantage of hearing some really first class singing and music. Mrs. Dupuis most kindly sang in the afternoon, Mrs. Alston played the violin at both performances, and Mlle. Hennequin, besides accompanying the violinist, also played some brilliant solos. Altogether the entertainment was a treat such as it is impossible often to get.

RECEIPTS	£	s	d	EXPENDITURE	£	s	d
Sale of tickets				Royalty paid for			
end entrance	12	14	0	using the play	1	0	0
Donation —				Printing and			
Mr. Spragg		2	6	stamps	1	0	6
				Carpenter		19	0
				The cost of 'buns'			
				for the tea		5	5
				Balance	9	11	7
	12	16	6		12	16	6

The Stitching Begins . . .

At Flitcham   The work which is being so willingly done in the village for the needs of the Army and Navy, progresses well, and completed garments keep coming in to the Vicarage. As this magazine goes to press, already there have been despatched to St. John Ambulance and to the Norfolk Needlework Guild, 86 garments; the latter Society sent a special appeal for help for the War, through Lady ffolkes. The next large parcel is to be sent to Queen Mary's Guild. The list of work already despatched is as follows:— 15 nightshirts, 10 shirts, 12 pr. socks, 4 pr. bedsocks, 29 pillow cases, 4 pillows, 3 suits of pyjamas, 9 bandages.

Castle Rising   In addition to the 278 articles made by the Castle Rising branch of the Guild, and announced in our last issue as sent to the depot, the following 124 articles have since been made and forwarded:- 12 belts, 6 prs. socks, to Devonshire House; 12 belts, 3 prs. stockings, to Mrs. Howard, for 60th Rifles; 5 mufflers to Lady French; 14 helmets, 20 prs. mittens, 10 prs. gloves, 2 prs. cuffs, to "Gloves for the Troops". The remaining 40 articles to Queen Mary's Guild and the Refugees. Parcels of clothing have also been sent to the Central depot for Refugees, and to Belgian Refugees at Handsworth, Birmingham.

And Roydon   The children of Roydon School have sent a parcel of socks to the Queen for distribution amongst the troops at the front, and have also collected 12/- which has been forwarded to Princess Mary for the sailors' and soldiers' Christmas Present.

Children help Miss Foster has originated a class of small boys
at Flitcham and girls who meet daily at the Vicarage; to make
cotton waste for hospital use.

Meanwhile everything possible was done to keep life as normal
as it could be for the children.

Prizes at The following is a list of children attending the
Roydon Roydon School who have obtained prizes given by
the Royal Freebridge Lynn Association:—
Hetty Barnes, 1st prize for button holes.
do.   2nd prize for marking.
Rachel Humphrey, 2nd prize for overall.
Dorothy Tuddenham, 2nd prize for darn.
Audrey Bolderstone, extra prize for socks.
Wallace Elsegood, 1st prize for drawing.
John Drew, 3rd prize for   do.
William Bunnett, 1st prize for essay.
Harry Thompson, 3rd prize for letter writing.

In spite of the war, it was thought unfair to deprive   **Treat**
the Sunday School of their treat. Messrs. Betts   **for Flitcham**
kindly lent a waggon, and the journey to Snettisham   **Sunday**
was made on Saturday 12th. The weather might have   **School**
finer, but the children's spirits were not affected by the rain.
The tea provided by Mrs. Brereton, Mrs. H. and T. Billing,
Miss Billing, Miss Bretten, Mrs. Clements, Mrs. Smith and Mrs.
Stephens, was much enjoyed in a comfortable club room at Snettisham.

Royal Sir Charles Cust, writing from Buckingham Palace
Praise on 16th Nov., said, "The King is very pleased to hear
how well the village of Flitcham has done in the matter
of recruiting." More than 1 in 9 of the total population is serving.

Reverend Charles Kent and the 'Breckland Magazine'

At the beginning of 1914 the Revd Charles Kent must have expected to spend his remaining active years quietly serving his Norfolk parishes of Merton, Thompson, Tottington and Sturston, and enjoying his favourite pursuits, fly-fishing, photography and local history. International events changed all this, and the war years were to prove some of the busiest and most eventful of his life.

From the first day of the war he threw himself wholeheartedly into organizing the local war effort. Then in January 1916 he devised a new way of maintaining contact between the men at the front and their relatives at home. With the help of Mrs de Grey regular gifts of tobacco, money, and Christmas puddings in season were sent out to the troops. In return they wrote back to the Rector with as much news as the censor would allow through. Mr Kent published their letters in his new 'Breckland Magazine', together with parish news and a local history article written by the Rector. The magazine was then sent out to the troops with the next batch of parcels. In this way the men at the front saw their own words in print and received news of their fellow Brecklanders in other parts of the globe. Revd Kent's war effort was not merely literary. In the last year of the war, at the age of 60, he undertook to go to France to help trace missing men.

The following extracts from the 'Breckland Magazine' tell us, month by month, the fortunes of some of the men who served from Mr Kent's parishes. There was perhaps a special closeness about these villages, for many of their menfolk were workers on the Merton estate of Lord Walsingham (de Grey) and knew each other well.

'The Breckland Magazine'

February 1916

The Earl of Leicester's letter commending our new magazine, and saying it was the very thimg needed in our country districts, has proved correct. Sold out and a second edition printed!

George Sturgeon. prisoner of war at Doeberitz writing home last month, said he had not received Mrs. de Grey's parcel for six weeks. Perhaps the Germans are eating the food we send.

Captain George de Grey did have a broken leg after all, but is making great progress. Speaking of Tottington's lost D.C.M., Capt. George writes: "Poor Sergt. Friston, Walter Hunt's grandson was killed — such a pity! He was our best young N.C.O., a very good leader and entirely fearless."

L.-Corporal Weeds has passed in a few months from Tottington Vicarage to the trenches in France. Writing the other day, he says "Many men have to be drawn out of the water and mud leaving their trench boots behind them. The most exciting night I have had out here was when a gas attack was going on and a soldier came in and said he had seen a spy on our parapet......we set out after the spy, up and down the trenches, looking with great caution over the top ...We could hear the Germans working quite plainly and when our men opened fire could hear them laugh."

Willie Thompson & Percy Baldwin wore, when at home, the distinguishing badge of 'bomb thrower', so evidently our lads from playing cricket early have proved as good at throwing the bomb as the cricket ball.

Walter & Cyril Watson & Albert Pipe represent Breckland in the fighting line at sea. The former too has been in most of the naval battles — the battle of the Bight, the sinking of the *Blucher*, and others. In a letter to the Rector he gave a vivid description of his destroyer, H.M.S. *Laforey*, dashing about in the midst of shot and shell.

Sidney Sturgeon has been home from the Dardanelles and hospital at Malta, where he recovered from a bad attack of dysentery. He won't forget Sulva Bay in a hurry. The bad organisation, as well as 'inertia', which Sir Ian Hamilton spoke of, is responsible for much. No water, and intolerable thirst! Poor Sidney had to run six miles to the firing line with his kit and entrenching tools without water. An intolerable thirst made him and others pull two dead Turks out of a water-hole and drink! They chanced the result, so terrible was their suffering. Dysentery followed. All our 4th were either killed, wounded or sick.

Leo Crane, who from a sick-bed became the hospital orderly, is now enjoying a good time. He writes from Malta, "Such a pretty place and warm climate. It was lovely here Christmas Day, with the sun shining beautifully. The nurses waited on us. After the dinner we were given a churchwarden pipe, tobacco and cigarettes, and then after the interval, a concert — the best I have ever heard. I know which hospital Bertie Baldwin is in - the other side of the grand harbour ... when on day duty I shall go and see him."

Sergeant Tuddenham, I am sorry to say, is in hospital suffering from gas and trench feet. He writes, "We had a rough time on Dec. 19th and 20th. We were gassed and the shells came as thick as hail. We lost over 100 men. I again thank God for bringing me through."

March 1916

James Kenny is no longer in the National Reserve but is Rifleman Kenny of the Rifle Brigade. When last heard of he had landed at Bombay, India.

Capt. George de Grey, also writing from Bombay, says "They (the Turks) got me at the end of the first day at Ctesiphon. I think I was peppered by a machine-gun, for two bullets hit me at identically the same moment; one broke my left shin-bone, but not badly. I was sent back to India straight away ..." He also says, "There is nothing in the world to beat the Norfolk man. He's worth four townsmen. The great thing about him is he never gets rattled or fussed."

Sergt. Hurring & Driver Arthur Macro, from whom, when in France, we used to hear constantly are now silent. Their wives too are in suspense. We know pretty well where they have gone, but evidently the authorities wish to keep their whereabouts a secret.

Driver Farrier G. Leeder, writing from France, says, "We are having some winter weather here now. I was thinking of the people of Tottington being in Church while we boys were up at the line of fire with shells screaming over our heads. It is a shame to see houses and churches blown to pieces."

Pte. Rowland Flatt, writes from France saying that the section of front line trench his brigade (Canadians) are holding has been the scene of heavy fighting. Over a frontage of 1,000 yds there lay by repute 35,000 dead French soldiers as they fell over 12 months ago. They lay in rows as they advanced in attack formation in front of barbed wire — their plush red trousers and blue tunics distinguish them as a famous first line corps.

April 1916

Capt. George de Grey. We are proud to record that the heir to the Merton Estate has been rewarded with the Distinguished Service Order. The London Gazette announces, "For conspicuous gallantry in the performance of his duties as adjutant; he repeatedly crossed fire-swept zones in order to take orders, send up ammunition, and direct reinforcements, until he was severely wounded. His cool bravey had twice previously been brought to notice."

Major Hines writes from Happisburgh, where he is officer in command of defence works. Of course of these he may not speak. German mines drifted near the shore, so the Major ordered the troops under shelter while he and another officer went to explode one. Major Hines hit it with a rifle at 200 yds. and it exploded; but the concussion was terrific, breaking windows and shaking houses while pieces of iron were hurled a mile or more.

Sergt. Hurring & Driver Arthur Macro, have been sent to the relief of General Townshend at Kut-Amara in Mesopotamia. The latter writes, "After a long time we are allowed to write letters. I am thankful to God that I have been spared through all the fighting we have done. I had the worst Xmas I ever had. This is a wild country, no roads, no trees, nor anything but a little river that is of any good. This is where we get our drinking water from. Sometimes it is all mud, but we are thankful to get that. We have been fighting ever since we landed. I am sorry to say my section officer was shot through the heart. He was such a nice young fellow... On the 7th we beat the enemy, they left several hundred dead on the field; but on the 21st it was awful. It poured with rain night and day. There were many poor fellows died in the mud and there was an armistice for six hours to bury them.

Lieut. R. E. Brassey writes from the Greek Serbian frontier, "There no Bulgars within 40 or 50 miles, the distance to the frontier. But you never know what they may be up to, so we have to keep a sharp look-out and patrol the country. Very useful work, also making maps and getting to know the country, for roads are few and far between ...The climate is extraordinary. For instance yesterday and the day before were as warm as a June day in England, while today it's enough to freeze an elephant! The poor horses feel it dreadfully. I am now acting as transport officer. It is rather a nice job, as you are more or less on your own and you get extra pay. Remember me to all."

Leo Crane, from St. Andrew's hospital, Malta, "All the men that come here are well looked after, while those poor fellows who die have a full military funeral and flowers always on their graves. I think the new magazine is a great success, much better than the old one ...... I often think on a Sunday of the Merton people walking peacefully to Church, while the sick and wounded are all around us with awful wounds..."

Rowland Flatt, It is with deep regret we have to announce the fourth death at Tottington on behalf of King and country. Rowland Flatt, of the 19th Canadian Battalion, was killed in action on March 11th, a bullet passing through his body causing instantaneous death. A comrade writes a touching letter, saying, "He was always cheery, even when others were gloomy. He was one of those men who could least be spared."

George Howard, sent home wounded from the Dardanelles, is now back in Egypt. "We are now close to a Norfolk Regiment, and I have seen one or two of the boys from Watton."

May 1916

Capt. George de Grey D.S.O. We have just had a letter from him saying his leg is mended, and that his sick leave ended on Apr. 22nd. Also he thanks everyone for their kind congratulations.

Rifleman James Kenny writes from Agra, India. He says the heat is increasing and the temperature is just on 100 degrees. As an old soldier, James has had all the native cooks placed under his charge, nor are these Indian cooks very easy to control.

Lieut. Brassey writes a cheery letter from a cosy camp on the frontier about Salonika, "We have seen several German patrols, but not near enough to have a go at them. We saw them being shelled by the French, and two French planes chasing a Taube firing with a maxim gun. They came right over, it was most exciting. The French bagged four Taubes, which was some consolation. The new Breckland Magazine is most interesting, as it gives all the doings of the Merton boys at the Front."

Charles Hancock writes from France most cheerful letters, but the Record Office still persists that he was killed some months ago. We have sent his letters and assured them that he writes regularly once a week. Apparently all in vain, since his widowed mother has now received forms to fill up and state her claims on the loss of her son.

Pte. Drew, our late postman, was at home some time ago and paid us a visit to give his experiences in the trenches. In spite of the mud, the damp, and great hardships, he has been quite as well and even better in health than when he used to come round with our letters.

Lce.-Corporal Weeds, our Reader, has been removed from a London Hospital to the Norfolk & Norwich Hospital. Apparently he suffered terrible hardships when on special duty with two privates. For some days they remained close to the German lines, standing or crouching in water. This resulted in an internal chill and accounts for a strong man like Mr. Weeds succumbing to hardship.

Pte. George Howard sends some charming post-cards showing the sights of Egypt ... George now cooks for the boys and is up every morn at 4 a.m. He says it is hot work under an Egyptian sun, with the sand and flies into everything.

Pte. S. H. Hunt, R.A.M.C. describes his landing at Sulva Bay: "We had a lively reception from the Turks, shells bursting all round us, bullets whizzing past, and Turks up in the air dropping bombs. We made a rush for it and one fellow beside me was wounded in the thigh, so I threw my kit down and helped to carry him to a place of safety and dressed him... Another time I was going through the camp when I heard a shell coming and just dropped in time. I closed my eyes and quite thought to have been blown to atoms. It covered me with sand and the men of the unit were surprised to see me get up unhurt."

June 1916

Pte. Percy Baldwin writes after a long silence, "I am sorry not to have written before. We have had a rough time of it lately. We only came out of the trenches on the night of the 11th after a sojourn there of 21 days. The position we hold at the moment is a very important one, which has been the scene of many a hard fight by the French.

Pte. Ernest Harrowing, writing from Egypt, where he is with Leo Crane and George and other boys from this part, "It is very hot out here and seems a long time since we had a winter, but wherever I go I shall never forget Gallipoli, that was a hot shop if you like. I must congratulate you on the new magazine, I look forward to it every month. I am glad to hear of the improvement at Tompson in getting an organ. I often think of a Sunday of the people all going to Church as we used to do, but out here you hardly know Sunday from any other day......"

Rifleman James Kenny, writing from Agra, India, "I don't want it to get much hotter, for it is 100 in the shade, and with the mosquitoes at night it is not so very pleasant. Most of the Battalion have gone to the hills, only 100 left here and in the fort. Not much life, except a whist drive and cribbage match every week at the R.A.T.A. also a concert weekly..."

July 1916

Capt. George de Grey D.S.O. writes "Many thanks to Merton, Tottington, Tompson and yourself for your congratulations. It was awfully kind of you all to send them. I am quite mended now and hope to go back to Mesopotamia before very long...Unfortunately Kut has gone, and with it the remains of the 2nd Battalion. I don't think there can have been more than 250 of them left. It is absolutely sickening to think of one's old regiment being prisoners."

Sergt. Victor Hurring, writing to his wife, says, "I must tell you a little piece of news, although I hardly like to. You nearly lost your humble servant. I hold the record of the Tigris river. I fell overboard. It was an accident which nearly cost my life, but not quite. I got out of it. I am at present the luckiest man in this part of the world."

Driver Arthur Macro, on the banks of the Tigris, writes to his wife, "We all wish we had never left France. The climate is most trying, at first heavy rain and floods, now dreadfully hot, and the flies are awful, not a tree or any shade, only what we make ourselves. We are up against a strong force of Turks, but they are a dirty ragged lot. On April 23rd, when we had our Field Service at 6 p.m., just as the sun was going down, not a shot to be heard, it seemed like a peaceful Sunday at Tottington. But it was not peaceful for long. Soon the shells began to fly about and the guns to thunder..."

Pte. Fred Bone of the Cyclists has quite grown into a fine soldier. He likes the life, it agrees with him, and we hear it is his intention to stay in the army.

Pte. Leo Crane, now in Egypt, writes, "The game of waiting day after day, and never seeing a Turk gets on one's nerves, as we have to go through the same routine as if they were facing us, I shall be glad when the old Turks come along for a scrap..."

Pte. George Sturgeon, a prisoner in the hands of the Germans, has been moved to Libau, and then back again to some other internment camp near Doeberitz.

Pte. G. E. Howard, has been doing the Pyramids. He writes "I was thinking of Tompson on Easter Sunday, wondering how you were getting on with the Bishop. Not often a bishop gets there! Have you ever visited the Pyramids? Isn't it wonderful how they were put up? We had to take our boots off to go inside, and I was pleased when we got out again; it was awfully hot inside...I have had enough of the desert to last me some time, Tompson is better."

August 1916

Driver Arthur Macro has sent us a long account of the attempt to relieve Kut. He concludes, "Everything has been against us, floods and rain, sandstorms and tormented by flies. We lost one man with cholera — I hear the Turks have got it bad. The boats are busy bringing the sick from Kut. I should like something to make drinks with, as it is the chief thing in this hot country."

Pte. Arthur Thorpe has met a soldier's death in the great Somme battle, and Tottington has given her fifth son in the service of the country. The five honoured names are in the order they fell — Perkins, Warby, Friston, Flatt and Thorpe. R.I.P.

Pt. Sidney Sturgeon, has gone on a course of bombing for a few days somewhere. We are glad to hear of Sidney, he was a splendid bowler and in throwing the cricket ball, and ought to turn out a first-class bomber.

Pte. George Howard, is in hospital with an attack of dysentery. He writes, "This hospital is quite close to the Canal, so we can see all the boats going by. It was a good thing our transport was so near the canal, as I don't think many of us knew how to swim before; now it is quite a sight to see us all in the water swimming about when work is done."

Lieut. Brassey, writing from somewhere near Salonika, says, "I am sharing a tent with a machine-gun officer, pitched under an apricot tree which does the double purpose of keeping the sun off and supplying us with food, as the apricots are ripe. Things are fairly quiet just now."

September 1916

Pte. Percy Dalton writes, "I was very pleased to get the postal order, and pleased also to know the people at home never forget us. I was wounded on July 7th, at Ovilliers, making an attack on the German trenches. We went over at 8.30 a.m., and started to walk to the enemy trenches 500 yds away. We did not get 40 yds before they opened fire on us in every direction. Nearly all our officers were killed before 50 yds were gone. Our Colonel was killed, having 8 bullets through him. Our losses were very heavy only two left in my platoon, and only 9 of the company of 250."

Pte. George Howard, is out of hospital and has rejoined the Norfolks· He writes "The parcel of cigarettes reached me safely. I distributed them to the boys...We have had another move further up the canal. The Turks are not so very far off, but I am afraid they don't like the idea of coming too close, as we have got some heavy stuff waiting for them."

Pte. Leo Crane, who has been down with dysentery, is about again. He writes, "I lazed about the camp for some days, trying to stick it and not report sick, but it got my master. When the doctor came round, he sent me to Port Suez. I was so bad there, that the doctor said I must go to Cairo. When we got to Ismailia, we were changed into the main hospital train running from Port Said to Cairo, which is fitted up splendidly. The fast of Ramadan is on now — the people fast till 7 p.m. when a gun fires, and then they may eat. It is so nice to have a clean bed under one."

Pte. George Sturgeon, prisoner of war, writes that he is all right being well looked after by Mrs de Grey. But for her parcels, reading between the lines, he would be face to face with starvation.

Rifleman James Kenny writes in the sweltering heat of Agra, India, "Half the men are in hospital. Last Sunday eight men were carried out of my room with fever."

Victor Blanchflower has joined Princess Patricia's reinforcements at McGill University, Canada. Well done!

October 1916

Sergeant Hurring writes from Mesopotamia, "I am fairly well in this awful heat, which yesterday was 122 degrees in the tent, and then the plague of flies! I don't know how many I've eaten. I only get a sleep when I am properly exhausted, for at night you get the malarial mosquitoes, scorpion spiders, scorpion centipedes and beetles. I have been some time answering your letter, which by the way was in my pocket when I fell into the Tigris. With so much work, I never have the energy to sit or lie down to write a letter. I've got 157 wagons to keep in repair, and have two British wheelers and three Indians to help, and as they are all British-made wagons, you can safely say they are all complete wrecks."

Pte. E. H. Hunt, R.A.M.C, writes from Africa, though nothing is said of the fighting, "We are in German East Africa now. We left Egypt on Good Friday last, travelling by water to Mombasa, then by the Uganda railway as far as Kajiado. After a few days here, we started on our adventurous trek with oxen convoys. We walked over 200 miles through burning sun and dust; sometimes we had to do 30 miles at a stretch over the waterless desert, but we all enjoyed it. The most exciting part was, when we bathed at night, to hear the lions roar, and other wild beasts. We had to burn big fires to keep them away ... It is an ideal spot. Fruit, flowers, birds, butterflies, all on a magnificent scale. Hyenas and leopards came through the camp the other night. The natives are curious. It costs them nothing for clothing."

Lce.-Corporal Fred Bone. It has been our sad duty to chronicle month by month the passing away in action of the splendid Tottington lads, and this month with deep sorrow we record the eighth. Fred Bone was a real Norfolk lad, sturdy and strong...In his first battle, almost at the first shot, he meets a soldier's death. Fred was among my first confirmation candidates at Tottington, at his own request, and so I fervently write — R.I.P.

Pte. Tom Jessup has been wounded badly, having exchanged from the Norfolks into the Fighting Fourths. He writes, "We went into the trenches on Sept. 14th, and the next morning had to attack...I didn't get very far before they dropped me to the ground. I managed to get to a shell-hole ... stopped there for a time and thought what a funny country I was in, as there were shells going in every direction and machine-guns firing. Well, I started to get the things off I had with me and it seemed as if I was cut in half! The bullets went in my left side and came out the right. The doctor told me more than once how lucky I was to see England again.'

November 1916

Pte. Percy Baldwin, who was wounded in August, writes, "I have to go before a Medical Board to see if I shall be fit for active service, but I fear I have a stiff leg for good. Thank you for sending the postal order....I wonder why some people said we were better off than them, when Mr Walter Nunn asked them to give a bob ... Our pay is about a shilling a day, and for this we offer our lives, while up here the men are earning in munition works from £5 to £20 a week."

Driver Charles Hancock, writing from France, says he is getting very home-sick; "I am just longing to see you all again, and the dear old church, and have a game of cricket. I am sorry to hear of poor Mr Hanner and Willie Thompson, Fred Bone and the other boys killed or wounded. Give my love to all my old friends..."

Pt. Tom Jessup writes, "I am getting on well after going through another operation last Monday, and they found a piece of something which was causing all the pain. Now I can rest much better."

Rifleman James Kenny writes "The Viceroy comes to Agra on Oct. 4th. I am to be one of the guard at his quarters. It all means extra duty, and with half the battalion in the hills we don't want that."

December 1916

Driver Arthur Macro writes from Mesopotamia, "There has not been much doing all through the hot weather here...We had the Bishop of Nagpur, India, to preach to us on Sat. Sept. 9th, as he had come to consecrate the graves of the poor fellows who have died for their country and are buried beside the Tigris ...Thank God I am keeping well. I saw in the Breckland Magazine you were starting a fund for the repair of the bells. I should like to help, and so am sending a pound by my wife for you."

Lieut. Brassey writes from the battle line above Salonika, "We have been kept pretty busy on this front for the last six weeks. I expect you've seen in the papers how the Bulgars advanced across the plain up to the Struma...I had a splendid view of the last battle when our troops crossed the river and drove the Bulgars out of the plain into the foot hills on the other side. Through a telescope I could see our troops advancing and the Bulgars retiring. Our guns played havoc amongst them; some put their losses at 10,000...."

Pte. T. J. Drew, our late postman, has been in hospital in France, but improving fast.

Pte. Leo Crane, writes from Egypt, "I am glad to say it is much cooler than it was, but still not a drop of rain has fallen since last April. Major Revd Gardiner is our chaplain here... He has been very good to our men and has obtained a piano for our Recreation Hut so that we can have music on Sundays and a sing-song during the week...I went down to Alexandria for a week and saw a lot of Turkish prisoners come in. Some Germans amongst them looked well and were big men, but the Bedouins looked like tramps, and were a heap of rags."

Pte. Sidney Sturgeon writes, "I did not go through a course of bombing, that was a mistake. I went through a course of Bloke's gun, and passed out first class."

January 1917

Rifleman James Kenny, writes from Agra, "We have had the Viceroy here on a visit...Everything went off quietly, but we had to stand to arms day and night all the time he was here, as the Mohammedan festival was on, and nearly every year there has been a disturbance, but they did not clash with the Hindus this year. Now I am back at my old job. These native cooks take a lot of watching — they are all rogues."

Pte. Ernest Oldfield, 8th Norfolks, writes, "Although I have not been out here long, I have experienced a good bit, as I have been in the trenches four times. I have heard that poor young Walter Hunt has died from his wounds. I am sure those who lose their dear ones out here have my sincere sympathy. It does seem a bit hard when you see your mate cut down beside you. However it is best to look on the bright side and be prepared for anything."

George Carrier jun. has joined H.M.S. *Kildonan Castle* — converted of course into a fast cruiser. George has had some exciting times and escapes from torpedoes, of which I may not write.

Farrier George Leeder writes, "Our worst trouble is to keep our feet dry. We are having a rest now, as we have been on the Somme twice. It is a proper wild country, this no-man's land, and one can see for miles and miles and no one but troops going up and down."

Farrier Willie Anthony, writing from Haynes Park, "This is a truly awful camp nothing but deep mud, and seven miles from any town. We have about 700 horses and mules here, so there is plenty of work...."

Albert Pipe A.B. (location unkuown), "Please convey my hearty thanks to the kind people of Merton for the P.O., which I was quite surprised to receive. We in my ship escorted over forty thousand in one week — one among fourteen ships."

Pte. T. J. Drew had his Xmas box from Merton Rectory as if he had been doing his rounds. He writes, "Thanks indeed for P.O. and Xmas box; I hope it will be the last out here, and that next year I shall be at home with the wife and children. It was nice to be remembered by Merton, as I haven't heard yet of anything from Watton. So remember me to all at the Rectory, and may I be spared to come round again."

Pte. R. Leffley writes, "You ask me what I have been doing? Well we were in the big Push at the start, and also several times later. After a bombardment, every place looks the same, trenches wrecked in, trees like bare poles, and the ground like the top of a pepper box. The smell of gas is not always unpleasant. One kind smells like a room where apples have been stored for some time. I have only been out of range of the German guns three times."

W. Watson A.B. writes, "We have been having beautiful weather for this time of year. I saw Albert Pipe the other week. He came alongside in a boat. I got ashore at Xmas, just to stretch my limbs.

Pte. George Howard, writing from Egypt, "Just received the New Year's gifts, P.O. from the people of Tompson, and your two plum puddings I got about a week ago. One was handed over to H. Kenny to divide among the boys. The mince pies followed. I went round with them to the boys; they laughed when they saw me coming, but they didn't know what I was bringing along..."

March 1917

Driver Arthur Macro writes from Mesopotamia, "I had a much better Xmas than last year. We had some nice gifts from India, for which ladies out there raised funds. They sent hams, and cakes and puddings. There is not much time now for writing, for the time has come to fight, now that the hot weather has gone. Now it is all mud ... The Turks often send their big shells over us and I think my last hour has come and thoughts fly homewards...

Pte. George Sturgeon who has been so long a prisoner in Germany now writes from Friedrichsfeld, yet there is nothing in the letter to tell us how things are. "When I read your letter it cheered me up a lot....I am quite well and hope to see you all again soon now. I expect Merton is a bit dull now the boys are away."

W. Watson we are pleased to hear has just been promoted leading seaman on H.M.S. *Lapwing*. He writes, I got this promotion on Jan. 1st, so I began the year well. We have to be on the look-out for mines every minute. We call them 'footballs', though I should not care to kick one. The Germans are going a bit far with submarines, but they will get it in the neck again."

The Rector has sent his name to the Bishop and Mr Neville Chamberlain for National Service.

Lord Devonport has put us on our honour to obey his food allowances. Intense privations await us if we do not obey orders.

April 1917

Major de Grey, D.S.O. has been taking part in the victorious advance in Mesopotamia and the capture of Kut... He has been again wounded - we are glad to say not seriously - in the shoulder.

Pte. Victor Blanchflower writes, "I am really off to France. I am going into the Canadian Record Office of casualties, but hope later to get into the trenches."

Sergt. Hurring writing to his wife, says, "We are on the move again... I have seen Major de Grey. He was in the same camp as I was. We had quite a lnog chat together about Merton and things in general. He was very pleased to see me ... Just now it is very cold, and I am thinking when we all meet again in Merton, we shall all be talking at one another in French.

Pte. Ernest Oldfield writes, "I have been transferred from my battalion to the R.E.'s for road-making, a great necessity just now, so that the boys may use them and keep pushing the enemies back. [Ernest used to work on our roads.] Although still in the danger zone, I like this job better than being in the trenches ... It makes anyone think who has been through it."

George Carrier R.N. was at home for a few days lately. It is wonderful what the training has done for him. He has grown into a fine lad, a splendid specimen of the British Navy.

May 1917

Pte. E. Harrowing writes, "...I am sorry not to have received the New Year's gift of the Merton people. Perhaps it is owing to me moving about so much. I am now in a convalescent Home at Cairo, getting my weight back, which I have lost. I had an outing last Saturday to the Citadel and Ali Mosque Mohamed."

Pte. G. Leeder, writes from France to his wife, "You just ought to see these villages, they are all blown away level with the ground ... The Germans are blowing the roads and railways up, and he does not stop at that, for he is poisoning the water and leaving poisoned chocolate behind, but we are up to his games. Also he is taking all the young French women as they retreat, and leaving only the old people in the villages."

Pte. Sidney Sturgeon is marching up with the Reserves to the fighting line in Palestine. **Pte. H, Kenny** and others of our boys are also there, so we shall soon have their impressions of the Holy Land.

Pte. Victor Blanchflower, with the Canadians, writes, "A line to let you know I have come safely through the big battle for the famous Vimy Ridge. One of my most embarassing moments was when I found myself imprisoned in a German dug-out, caused by an explosion taking place while I was bombing the dug-out. However I managed to extricate myself, but not till after I had been temporarily reported missing."

Driver A. Macro, "Everything this year is much better for us, ...but like you at home we are tired of the war, but we must stick it till the enemy is beaten."

Sergt. Hurring writes from before Kut, "I received your parcel yesterday very crushed, the tobacco gone and the cigarettes flat, but some were smokeable ... Major de Grey has gone up to the Front again. He looked very fit and said his wounds did not hurt.

June 1917

Pte. Sidney Sturgeon. Merton has been in great gloom through the death in action before Gaza of our promising young lad, Sidney Sturgeon, whose parents are much respected. Indeed great sympathy is felt for Mr. and Mrs. William Sturgeon who have given their four sons as soldiers. Arthur is in France, George is a prisoner in Germany, having been taken prisoner at Mons, Sidney has died in action for his country, and Reggie just eighteen years is a recruit. R.I.P.

Shoeing-Smith Willie Anthony writes on shipboard with the East African Expeditionary Force, "We are having a grand voyage... I am with several of the old boys from the Signal Co. R.E. at Watton, and Ralph Blake is on the same boat going to the same place. So I have plenty of pals. There are some lovely sights to see. I never thought there were such sights when I was at Tompson."

Driver George Howard sends the bad news, "It is with the deepest regret that I have to tell you of the death in action of poor Sid Sturgeon. He was put in charge of a section, and would have been corporal if he had got through safe. You may have heard details of the fighting, and how my regiment was cut up. I have been doing my bit, carting water to them; of course the camels took it throuh. I have just turned the horses off into a corn field, a great change after the desert.

Driver Arthur Macro, writes to his wife, "We are in Bagdad. Just a month ago we begun the advance — a bit rough going, but splendid weather and a lucky thing, as we had no tents ......The move was worked splendid. The Turks could not stick our shellfire, once we got them on the move ... I came through where poor Walter Friston was killed (Ctesiphon). Poor boy! I did think about him then; it is the oldest place out here." By the time this magazine is in the hands of its readers the Rector and Editor will have left for France, so he bids all "au revoir" for some months, and hopes everyone will profit as much as he will.

Rifleman James Kenny writes from India, "I thought I would wait to write until I was settled in our new station. It is not so nice as Agra, as being a frontier station there are no civilians...We are quite on the borders of Kashmir. The natives are much fairer, they would be quite white if they would only wash more often, but they seem to be afraid of water."

Late News. As I start on my journey news comes that poor George Sturgeon is no more. Neither I nor his parents had heard for long, and feared something was wrong. I had heard our Norfolk lads captured at Mons had been forced to hard labour on the Russian front and were suffering terribly. Can this be how George was done to death, a strong healthy lad? We can only assure Mr. & Mrs. Sturgeon that their sorrow is our sorrow, now and always. R.I.P.

July 1917

Pte. Arthur Sturgeon. We have a report that Arthur Sturgeon is seriously wounded. We pray that Arthur may be spared for the sake of his sorrow-laden parents.

Pte. Herbert Kenny writes to the Rector from the Holy Land, "No doubt you have heard about our losses and bad luck. I have lost my best chum, Sid Sturgeon. It was the worst battle I've been in...This is a lovely country. There are funny hills and holes about where we can hide our wounded. Gaza is a big place to look at, but I have not had the pleasure of going in to it. The corn looks lovely, but the damage is very great. The wild flowers also are very beautiful...

The Rector Off to the Front! Even the starting of the boat train was kept a dead secret until 6 p.m. the night before, because of German spies... I reached the fast steamer and went on board at 6.30 p.m. on June 22nd, and crossed to sunny France by the long sea route ....Although mine and torpedo lay in the treacherous waters, I had a splendid crossing ...... I am to do censor's work. These are the private and confidential letters of husbands to their wives and young soldiers to their sweethearts. The soldiers would rather an old man like myself read these.

Farrier Willie Anthony writes from South Africa, "Here we are in a rest camp, but not for long. There are mules out here, and I expect I shall get some rough ones to deal with. We are amongst the fruit gardens, so we get plenty of fruit. The natives are a funny lot of people. Ralph Blake is still with me and several Norfolk boys are here."

H. H. Prince Frederick Duleep Singh writes from somewhere in France that he has a pleasant job looking after a camp of artillery horses which have come down to rest and be cosseted after the severe winter and strain of the front. After about a month they return to their units fit and well. He also says that his brother has seen a good deal of Lord and Lady Walsingham in the South of France, who are very well.

Rifleman James Kenny writes, "You will see I have got to another place. We are on the furthermost British outposts of the Kashmir frontier... This is a beautiful place in a big pine forest. Our tents are not uniform, but just where we can stick them. Sometimes we have to cut down trees to get them up at all. The native tribes are not to be trusted. Only last Thursday two British officers were murdered just below our camp, so we are not allowed out of camp after dark, and only in groups during the day."

The late Pte. George Sturgeon. Mr & Mrs William Sturgeon have heard through the War Office that poor George died of pneumonia in a Russian hospital, and was buried in a Russian cemetery.

September 1917

Sgt.-Major FredPerkins. In the honour of the war, Tottington, as in most things, leads the way. Indeed, if we include Major George de Grey, since Westmere was his country home, Tottington easily beats the neighbourhood, with D.S.O. for Major de Grey, and Sgt. Friston, D.C.M., and now the Military Medal won by Sgt.-Major Perkins, who by his gallantry on the field of battle, has risen to the chief place among non-commissioned officers.

Sergt. Hurring of Merton, is another who is winning distinction having been thrice mentioned in despatches, and recommended for a Distinguished Service Medal.

Driver Arthur Macro. We are now sorry to learn that the terrible sandstorms have temporarily injured his eyes. He is expecting a month's leave to recuperate in India.

Pte. S. H. Hunt, R.A.M.C., writing from East Africa, says, "There is still a campaign going on out here - a kind of guerrilla war - but there is much talk of finishing it this season. I have had some exciting times ... One place we came through was infested with lions, which could be seen in the daytime. We used to make platforms up a tree, then get an ox or a donkey that was no further use, then wait up the tree with a flashlight. After dark we would hear the lions roaring and snarling, which made us feel as if we were in the Zoo. One night our officers shot three. There are elephants not far from where we are, but they are more difficult to get. They make a road through the jungle just as if two or three steam rollers had gone along. A little time ago two of my officers and myself camped out. The place was alive with man-like monkeys and as big. They were so human we could not shoot them...There are also plenty of zebras, leopards, rhinos and giraffes out here."

George Carrier R.N. has gone on a secret voyage, and has not been heard of since July 19th.

S.C.S. Willie Anthony writes from East Africa, "I am feeling myself again, as I have had twelve days in hospital with Malarial fever. The climate is a bit too hot for a white man. I am in the workshops here. There are very few horses, nearly all mules, for the horses can't stand the heat and the flies... Kind regards to all Tompson people. Please excuse scribble, the flies and mosquitoes are enough to eat one."

The Rector is very happy in his work with the B.E.F. in France. He is now beginning to know the soldiers, and often has a friendly game of chess or draughts with them in the evening.

I have just opened the 'Watton Times' to find that the wrangle about the right of way through the locked gate, begun last May, is still going on in August and likely to continue! Fancy in war time! all these precious hours about a right of way, about which there never was ancient way for vehicles, only for foot passengers.

October 1917

Rte. H. Ripe writes from Palestine, "I am glad to say my wounds have healed up nicely. I am pleased to hear you think it is God's will we should clear the Turks out of this land. If the tales are true they are treating the natives and Jews very badly. I saw Herbert Kenny a little while ago, and he was quite well... When we first advanced up here the country looked like Blighty, now it looks just like the old desert, not a blade of grass or corn, nothing but dust."

Pte. E. Harrowing writes still from Egypt, "I am very well and 'in the pink', right up in the desert now. I have not come across any of the boys, only Ernie Bowman, who used to drive the mail cart from Thetford to Watton and Shipdham. I am dreadfully sorry to hear about Sid. Sturgeon, and it is so sad for his people. Merton will not be the same ever again."

The Rector. Owing to the war our English people and stray wounded and convalescent soldiers are quite neglected in Italy and Southern Europe. The Bishop of Gibraltar has asked the Rector to leave the B.E.F. for the winter months and go and act as spiritual head of the English congregations at Venice, Turin, and Milan, residing at Milan where the largest number are. The Rector has not seen his way to accept as yet, owing to the high cost of living in Italy, and also to the cold of Northern Italy, but is further considering the offer.

We are adding to the female population here very fast. Khaki girls are now coming across in swarms, caring little for the danger of U-boats with the usual British pluck.

December 1917

Pte. Leo Crane writes from the Holy Land, "I saw Dick Harrowing a few weeks back at the station on my return from leave. I hear from George Howard and Fred Boughen now and again, as they are both near up Gaza way. It is splendid here now — not too hot, and we are getting a bit of a breeze, only it lifts the sand. I am glad 'Breckland' continues. It is a great help to us to know how our pals are doing scattered about the world."

Corpl. James Kenny writes from the Indian Frontier, "We are having damp cold weather and heaps of rain. The mud at the Front is appalling. The soldiers come in plastered. There is not much light or encouragement. We must wait patiently till the Americans are ready."

January 1918

Farrier Driver G. Leeder writes, "We are having some winter weather here ... Belgium is the worst place I have been in. We always heard say "Remember Belgium," but never shall I forget it. I have walked round the Cathedral of Ypres, and wondered if ever it would be restored."

Corporal James Kenny writes "I left the hills on Oct. 4th for Halkot, and left again on Oct. 30th for this place. This is a nice place, not many troops. We are not allowed into the city. It's a large place, walled all round, with 13 gates, but I hope before we leave it will be in bounds, as I want to see the famous Golden Temple. The King, when visiting India, made a visit. Everyone has to take off their boots, and leave matches, tobacco etc., outside..."

Driver G. E. Howard writes from Palestine, "Things have been changing lately here, as no doubt you have heard. John Turk is on the run. I thought that when we got into Gaza we should see a fine town. Well it is nothing but a heap of ruins. The Turks had taken all the woodwork off the buildings to make their trenches with. I don't think there are any doors in Gaza now...My word, we are pestered with flies up here, — some of Jack Turk's pals, but I wish he had taken them with him."

Farrier Willie Anthony writes from the African colony just conquered from the Germans,"We have been giving them pepper here lately. You will be sorry to hear that Ralph Blake has been invalided down to South Africa...The climate did not suit him... The scenery is very pretty, but it is an awful country for fighting in, as round here it is nearly all bush. The rainy season will soon be here. It does not rain like with us, but it falls down in sheets. I have got used to the black boys. They were a funny lot at first. We have a lot in the workshop here. I quite understand them now...I shall be glad to see the old place once more."

February 1918

Pte. A. Sandcraft who was reported missing on Sept. 30th, is, we hear, wounded and a prisoner of war.

The Rector spent a very pleasant Xmas-tide and New Year and enjoyed some plum pudding sent out from England. I don't think the French have any idea of how to make them; also he had so many tins of tobacco presented to him that for a long time he will not want to buy any.

March 1918

Driver Arthur Macro has gone on leave to India, and landed at Bombay. His eyesight is improving,..He says it was a joy to sleep once more in a comfortable bed after three years of the hard ground.

Pte. Scarfe Hunt, R.A.M.C. writing from German East Africa says, "I think that the campaign out here will soon be finished, perhaps before you get this letter. I am looking forward to getting home soon, as there is an order that all those who have been out two years and over are to have leave. It's awfully hot out here. In some parts they have heavy rains, but where I am we have only had one shower since last March."

S.C.S.A. Willie Anthony writing in November last says, "I have been in hospital again with malarial fever. I was sent up to a place called Morogora, to a convalescent camp among the mountains. It was beautiful up there, with water flowing down made the scenery lovely. We saw bush fires every day - miles of country all ablaze. There are all sorts of wild beasts in this country - monkeys as big as I am and tremendous snakes."

The Rector felt he was getting too old [to go to Italy]...The spirit is willing, but the flesh is weak...Besides the necessaries of life are not obtainable, and one has to be content with bully beef and army rations, which are all right for young men's teeth.

April 1918

Corpl. G. E. Weeds writes, "The 21st of March 1918 will be my last day in the army, that being the date of my discharge." Corpl. Weeds has all our sympathy, for those early days in the trenches quite broke down a strong vigorous man, while to be sent there again in spite of the best medical opinion was fatal.

Willie Anthony writes, "I have had another attack of fever, but have kept out of hospital. This is an awful climate for white men, although a pretty one...We have to wear pads to keep the sun off our spine and big pith helmets .... We have plenty of work and I have learnt a lot since I have been in the army... The niggers are good boys; I have learnt their language. They tell me how the Germans used to ill-treat them. Most shamefully. Now they are quite happy and beg in English not to give them back to the Germans. You can lead them, but they won't be driven."

Driver George Howard says, "We are seeing the sights of a lifetime. Have you seen the orange groves round Joppa? Wonderful. I have also been round the town, but you want someone to tell you its history."

The Rector. It is reported that the Germans by leaflets have threatened us with destruction by aeroplane bombs tonight. We are awaiting this terrible fate with much composure... our Good Friday and Easter were outwardly quiet, save for the hundreds of poor shattered mortals passing through and the fresh troops going up to the battle area.

May 1918

Pte. Arthur Sturgeon, we deeply regret, has been reported missing in the great battle... We can only pray and hope that Arthur will turn up again when the stragglers have come in or even as a prisoner.

Pte. F. Fletcher, writing under the date 2.4.18, says, "Things are fairly quiet here now, but we have been in a rough quarter, in fact as soon as I got back from leave I lost all my kit. I saw the King the other day, and he spoke some very kind words to our chaps. I hope this job won't last much longer, as Fritz is getting quite reckless, but he will be beaten in the finish."

The W.A.AC.s Miss Bennett (daughter of Mrs H.Buckle, Tompson) writes, "Just a few lines to let you know I have arrived in France. I have been here nearly ten weeks. Hilda Cully, of Merton came here a few days before me. We have a nice Chaplain. Last Saturday night three of the girls were baptised."

Staff-Sergt. V. G. Hurring writes from Mesopotamia, "It has been very cold here lately. Just fancy waking up and finding the bucket of water for the morning wash a solid lump of ice in Mesopotamia! I saw some of the Norfolks last week and enquired about Major de Grey. They told me he was well again and at duty."

The Rector suddenly had permission granted to take his 'leave' at once.

June 1918

Pte. Arthur Sturgeon. We are glad to hear that Arthur is still alive, although a prisoner in Germany. Let us hope he will be treated more humanely than poor George.

Pte. Herbert Kenny writes a letter 'Damaged by immersion in sea-water through enemy action', "We still keep the Turks very busy, and before long shall have driven them to the other end of Palestine. This is a nice place with plenty of oranges and nuts. We go and get a sack full every day from the orange groves, but the nuts we have to buy... I have seen Herod's castle, now knocked to pieces by the Turks..."

Pte. Archie Blake writes from India, "I spoke of the various classes of education there are in the army. Well, I was fortunate enough to get my 2nd class certificate. I am getting ready for my 1st class... This study passes the time away, otherwise we should get very sick of doing nothing... I am trying to learn an Indian language, which is difficult owing to my limited knowledge of the grammar..."

Pte. A. Sandcraft, who was a prisoner of war in Germany, has arrived in London, and is in hospital at Camberwell.

Pte. Victor Blanchflower writes from France, "The weather has been exceptionally warm these last few days. I have had to stop work frequently, and visit a shady orchard to get a breath of fresh air...Our residence and office consist of a section or part of a farm house, and as you will know what experts the French are in coffee -making, you will understand how much we appreciate the fresh cream with which the farmer supplies us."

The Rector. We have had many difficulties to contend with in keeping 'Breckland' a going concern through the war. No matter to be printed is really allowed to pass [the Censor]. It was only by resorting to a subterfuge we were able to continue. The Rector wrote to Mr Fletcher...he was able to take out of the letters what was required to be published. ...nice to be in England once more.

August 1918

Pte. William Flatt has died for his country making the second of two brothers. In civil life he was butler to the late Prime Minister, Mr Asquith.

Corporal Best, writing from France, says, "We were all much struck out here by your article in the 'Breckland Magazine' about Tommies being tired of the war. We all agreed it was perfectly true, and quite different to what you see in the newspapers."

W.A.A.C. Matilda Quantrill writes from Aldershot, "I expect you saw in the papers all about the royalties' visit to Aldershot. We had a grand review by the King and Queen. The march past was a lovely sight...A few weeks ago we went through a drilling contest and I was one who passed. I was asked if I would volunteer as Drill-Instructor, but declined the offer. So now I am waiting at the Staff Table."

September 1918

Lce.-Corpl. James Kenny writesfrom India, "I have passed through a general Instructor's course, and came out top of our Battalion, so I am in hopes of getting away as Sergt.-Instructor for a native regiment raised for Mesopotamia... 120 in the shade, but I keep in good health."

Sergt.-Major F. Perkins has been for some time with the American soldiers who have come to France to finish their training... Judging by the way the Americans distinguished themselves in the second battle of the Marne, they have proved apt pupils..."

October 1918

Major George de Grey has recovered from his wound received in France. The Lieut.-Col. of the 1st Norfolks was unfortunately killed by his side...Major George is now in temporary command of the 1st Battalion.

Pte. Stephen Wright writes from Palestine that he has seen "bones supposed to be the bones of St. George...I have also been to Joppa....Antipatris..... Gaza, Askelon, Ashdod, Zebnah, Ahir, Ramleh, Ono, Jehud, but I have not yet been to Jerusalem. A word about the natives. They are the dirtiest, laziest lot I have have ever seen. They will steal anything they can lay their hands upon, and terrible liars."

The Rector. When you read this the writer will probably be commencing his work at the War Office. He is to seek the missing and lost!

November 1918

Pte. Victor Blanchflower writes a private letter from France, speaking of an interesting event to take place in the near future.

The Rector. At last I am settled down to my work at the War Office, searching records day after day and writing to poor anxious and bereaved mothers, wives, and sweethearts. My head often aches and throbs with the numberless piteous letters beseeching for news...A young girl 'Ivy' writes that her mother died two months ago and she is looking after six little brothers and sisters...

December 1918 (the final edition)

Peace! Armistice signed! the words were electric! The news first arrived at the War Office. In a moment or two the whole place was in an uproar. No more work was done that morning, it was impossible. Presently outside, cheers, shouting, bugles, and the noise of improvised musical instruments, girls rushed from houses of business and began dancing and footing it in the streets, men gathered at street corners to discuss the welcome news. A holiday was given to the people and schools...... Even the War Office gave notice all would be spared who wished to go, so after finishing one or two of the most important letters I retired to the Authors' Club.

POSTSCRIPT

As hinted in the November edition, there was a Merton wedding in store for Pte. Victor Blanchflower, and a grander London wedding for Major de Grey. The surviving men returned in due course to a hero's welcome. Their names, as well as those of the men who gave their lives, are recorded on the memorials of Merton, Thompson, and Tottington and Sturston. The last-named parishes are now in the Stanford Battle Area. The churches are abandoned and their war memorial stands in a lonely roadside spot between Merton and Thompson. The name of the Revd Kent stands proudly beside those of the men who 'served and returned safely' at both Merton and Thompson. His health suffered as a result of his war-time labours, but he continued to minister until his death in 1929.

These letters from the front are obviously much edited: by the men, who selected what the Rector wanted to hear, by Revd Kent, who prepared them for publication, and by the present editor who has selected only the most interesting passages from the many letters. There is, however, no reason to doubt their truthfulness, nor the remarkably steadfast and patriotic spirit of the men who wrote them.

Epilogue

After the War

The war ended; the troops came home and were at length demobilised, though the process was slow. (Revd Prichard of Knapton was not set free from his duties at Coltishall garrison until May 1919.) The relief was great, but then, as though the national suffering had not been sufficient, the early months of 1919 brought a serious outbreak of influenza. Amongst an already under-nourished population, the old and the very young were especially vulnerable. At Knapton the burials of Mrs Pain, aged 70, and Gladys Abbs, aged 3 months, were recorded for April 1919, and the officiating minister wrote, 'The health of the parish is indeed a cause of great anxiety, for in nearly every house the terrible plague of influenza has entered.'

Boards of Honour and War Memorials were a dominant concern during the post-war months, the raising of the necessary funds often taking years to complete. Garboldisham's Parish Magazine provides some typical entries for the period.

Garboldisham Roll of Honour, October 1920

We have at last been fortunate enough to secure photographs of all the Garboldisham men who gave their lives in the Great War. These have now been mounted and placed together in one large oak frame; the full names, Christian and Surname, of each, together with the date and place of his death, being written underneath. On the top of the frame itself, the following inscription is painted in red letters:

These are the photographs of the true and faithful men who, in the Great War, went forth from this place, for God and the Right, and returned not again. R.I.P.

The War Memorial itself was not unveiled until the June of the following year. There is a long and passionate account of the ceremony in the magazine for July 1921 which ends:

'And as we reluctantly leave this sacred spot and this beautiful monument, erected to the memory of the noble sons of Garboldisham, our hearts go out in thankfulness to God and to them for their noble example, and we murmur the hope that generations yet unborn will walk in their footsteps in service to their God, their King and their Country, and echo again and again in their hearts the exhortation of the Memorial, 'Praise God for these men of Garboldisham, who loved liberty more than life, and were faithful unto death.'

At the same time, however, normal parish life was returning. Major Denny D.S.O., whose previous feats had been on the field of battle, was to be seen scrambling to victory in the father's race at the School Treat held in his Garboldisham garden. The reading room was re-opened, school and choir outings took to motor transport, the Mothers' Union resumed its meetings and cricket was played again — albeit so badly that on one occasion Kenninghall scored a total of 35 runs, and won a crushing victory over Garboldisham by dismissing them for 24!

Finally, the Village Band broke its war-time silence.

♯♭♯   ♯♭♯

'The Village Band which, during the war,
had to lay their instruments aside, have now
made a fresh start. The younger members,
lately joined, are making such satisfactory
progress that the Band hope in a few months time
to be in a position to accept engagements.'

Erratum P.65 l.7 should read Pte. H. Pipe.

74